Nothing Great Is Easily Won-The Solomon Butler Story by David K. Sebben

Copyright 2023

Dedicated to my favorite athlete,

Leigha Nicole Sebben

Preface

My inspiration for this book came from the first book I worked on, <u>Rock Solid</u>: <u>Our History</u>, a collaboration with Doug Frazer and Rick Miers about the history of Rock Island High School. I was honored to be asked to contribute my photos and historical input about Rocky. My first knowledge about Solomon Butler came from reading about his record eight touchdowns versus Aledo back in 1914, listed in the Rock Island football program for many years, and thinking how a record from over 100 years ago could still stand. After doing a small story about Butler in the <u>Rock Solid</u> book, I knew his entire story had to be told. I was researching deeply into 100-year-old newspaper articles, emailing individuals in Kansas, Ohio, Colorado, Pennsylvania, Missouri, Alabama, New York, Michigan, California, Illinois, and Iowa that had information about Butler, countless hours in libraries, phone calls, and searching high and low on the internet. I ran into several dead ends, but most of the information discovered was eye-opening and at times, extremely emotional. I was heading down a path that hadn't been walked on in generations, if at all, and many of those footprints were disappearing. I learned more about Solomon than very few people knew, and I'll openly admit that I became emotional and angry at times when reading about some of the racial strife he had to endure as a youth and as an adult. Yet, he took it all in stride and he showed immense character and class always with his big smile. Please remember that many of the accounts are taken as they were written in his times, I have the utmost respect for him. I hope you enjoy reading about Solomon Butler and his life as much as I had researching him and writing this. Sol is the greatest athlete you've never heard about. Until now.

David K. Sebben

Sol Butler and Some Trophies

Nothing Great Is Easily Won- The Solomon Butler Story

By David K. Sebben

Chapters

Included is the book written by Sol and Ben Butler, _Three Years of High School Athletics_

Chapter 1- Civil War and Civil Unrest

March 4, 1839. An infant was born into slavery in Morgan County, Alabama, Benjamin Stephenson. At the age of 21, he was listed on the slave inventory after Stephenson's death in 1858. As was often customary in the time of slavery, he would take the last name of his owner, Arthur Stephenson. But when Stephenson passed away, the slaves, along with the property, were divided up among the children. Benjamin went to the Burleson family and was treated well, and took the last name of Burleson.

Jonathon Burleson   Source: David Burleson, great grandson of Jonathon Burleson

Jonathon Burleson owned vast amounts of acreage and a beautiful home, named Westview, in a valley near Flint Creek in northern Alabama. The plantation was constructed in 1840 and it was a prosperous farm, with cotton as the primary source of income.

Map showing Westview plantation, (center circle) drawn by Union soldiers   Source: David Burleson

Westview Plantation in Morgan County, Alabama   Source: David Burleson

By 1850, the plantation had grown to 11,000 acres and consisted of the overseer's house, a dozen slave cabins, a cotton press and gin house, barns, smokehouses, and a variety of shops to sustain the enterprising farm. By 1860, all but one of the Burleson's sons had left Westview. Five other sons and seven daughters had moved away to find their place in the South's prosperity. The once thriving farm was slowly falling into ruin and would continue to do so as the Civil War loomed. The Westview plantation would eventually be overtaken by Union Army troops and the belvedere room at the top would be used to monitor rebel movements. (*Westview survives to this day and is still owned by the Burleson family*)

Ben, and his brother, William, two years his elder, were both mule tenders at Westview and were planning their escape from the bondage of slavery and to seek refuge in the North. They were successful. On November 22, 1863, the brothers enlisted in the 2nd Iowa Infantry, Company "B" in Decatur, Georgia, with Ben signing on as an undercook and William as a foot soldier. (*Army records showed his name as Benjamin Bullison*).The brothers were involved in multiples stations (battles) in the South, and eventually joined with General Sherman's campaign to burn Atlanta and then on to Savannah, Georgia.

Actual flag carried by the Iowa 2nd Infantry

General Benjamin Butler

A list of stations that the 2nd Iowa Infantry were involved in

The 2nd Iowa ended its tour in March 1865, at Goldsboro, North Carolina, and traveled northward, eventually marched to Washington, D.C. to participate in the celebrations there. Due to his admiration for General Benjamin Butler, Ben Burleson saw the opportunity to change his last name and abandon his last ties to slavery. The soldiers of the 2nd Iowa would make their way to Davenport, Iowa where they were discharged from military service on July 20, 1865. (*It was rumored that Benjamin returned to Westview to meet with Jonathan Burleson to shake his hand and to express no ill feelings*)

In an interview from 1910, Benjamin Sr. talked about his time as a slave. "Sometimes, I think the old days is the best days, after all, and wish that I was back on the old plantation," Ben told a Hutchinson reporter. "I had never been sold. I was an honor slave. That is I was trusted a lot and I was the best cotton picker around. I picked 400 pounds of cotton every day," he said. "When the war began, old master was too old to enlist but all the boys and his brothers went to the war. I run the plantation for old master and got out three crops after the war opened. It was in 1863 when the Yankee soldiers was only six miles away that Master told me I'd have to go off and take the stock to the Confederate Army. He told me to take all the mules and other stock. I didn't want to get into any army, 'cause I knowed they were coming to help my people out. I never had no kick again being a slave, but I knowed there were a lot of my people that were being treated the same as dogs." Butler Sr. continued, "So I made up my mind I'd run off and I did. I made my way to the Yankee army and they sent me to Pulaski, Tennessee, and there I was made a soldier by the recruiting officer. They enlisted me as a cook for a company in the Second Iowa regiment on November 22, 1863."

"I never knew what it was to be sold," he continued on about his time as a slave. "I never learned to read or write, and I was determined to make sure my children would get an education."

Ben Sr. would eventually get a pension for several years as a Civil War veteran under the name Burleson, until he went to Washington to get his 'new' last name formally changed to Butler.

Benjamin Butler would eventually settle in the Memphis, Tennessee area, where in 1887, he would wed Mary Wellings, of Macon, Georgia, who was born a free woman in 1867. Ben was 48 years old and Mary was 20, and he worked as a sharecropper to provide for his new bride. The couple's first child, Anna, was born on March 6, 1889, with Benjamin Jr being born on August 9, 1892. March 9, 1892 saw a great civil unrest in Memphis as three prominent black businessmen were lynched. Tension persisted for many months and a local black newspaper, *The Headlight*, featured several stories detailing the lynching. Ida B. Wells, the editor, was away in Philadelphia working on another story, when a large white mob retaliated against her and her office, destroying everything inside. It was clear that she would have been killed had she been there.

Memphis in the late 1890's

Due to the tension and strife in the Memphis area at this time, over 6,000 black citizens, including the Butler family, left in 1892 to head west for better opportunities. Kingfisher, Oklahoma, over 500 miles from Memphis, was a community where numerous black families had migrated, seeking out a life from the hardships experienced in Tennessee. Yet, racial issues were tense in Kingfisher, with reports of "barbarous, inhuman, and ungodly treatment" of the local blacks. After several months of working a small farm, Ben and Mary welcomed their third child, Josephine, on January 20, 1894.

Solomon Wellings Butler, the last child of Ben and Mary Butler, was born on March 3, 1895 on a small farm near Kingfisher, Oklahoma. Sadly, discrimination and racial unrest found their way into this small community, and the Butler family moved to Wichita, Kansas in 1904, and enrolled the children in school. Again, racial segregation policies in Wichita forced the family to relocate again, and in 1907, they moved to Hutchinson, Kansas.

Chapter 2-The Hutchinson Years

Solomon Butler enrolled at the 4th Avenue Elementary School in September 1907, and it was here that he was first exposed to athletics, specifically football. The family was accepted into the community and became members of the Bethel AME Church at 1001- East 3rd Street. Benjamin Sr. became a member of the Grand Army of the Republic post. He had a shoeshine and "strawberry finish" drink stand in downtown Hutchinson and his mother took in wash to support the family. Despite his lack of education and 'social status', Ben Sr. was a highly respected member of the community.

Baseball would find its way into the youngest Butler's world in the summer of 1909. In September, he transferred to Maple Street Elementary School, where he continued to excel in football and was greatly admired by his peers. He was elected captain of the Central City grade school varsity eleven that won the city grade school championship. As each summer passed, he became increasingly better in football and baseball.

Maple Street Elementary School in Hutchinson, Kansas

The earliest known photo of Sol, taken in 7th grade

Source-Reno County Museum

On September 4, 1911, Solomon Butler and Clarence Phillips were the first black students to enroll at Hutchinson High School. At first, the predominately white student body did not accept them, but once they got to know them, they were deemed to be 'just like the rest of the guys."

SOLOMON BUTLER.

Hutchinson High School as it appeared when Butler attended

Butler as a freshman in 1911

The first game of the 1911 season was played against Stafford High School on October 7, with Butler starting as a freshman at the left halfback and safety positions. Yet, when Butler stepped onto the field, Stafford refused to play against a black opponent. He graciously removed himself from the game and Hutchinson High went on to win 5-4.

The following week saw the Hutchinson team travel to Lyons High School, where Butler and Phillips were met with more controversy.

"Lyons High objected to the playing of two Negros on the Hutchinson lineup, but Coach Don Yoeman stood pat and the men were played during the game. The stand by Lyons was poorly taken as the best athlete who has been on their teams for several years was a Negro." Source: *Hutchinson News*, October 16, 1911

When the game finally resumed, a battle ensued between Hutchinson's swiftness against Lyons steadfast defense. In the end, the teams played to a 0-0 tie.

Sterling, Kansas High School came to town on October 21 and were soundly defeated 34-11, with Butler scoring three touchdowns for 15 points. (*At this time in the sport, touchdowns were only awarded 5 points*). The Blue and Gold squad from Hutchinson traveled to Kingman on October 28, 1911 and unloaded a 37-3 trampling of the home team. A no huddle offense and a muddy field from the previous day's snow and rain contributed to the defeat of Kingman. An official at the game stated that Hutchinson was the "best high school team I ever saw." Butler scored four touchdowns.

Probably the most interesting game of the 1911 season was on November 11 when the "Salters" boarded the train for the 45-mile trek to Stafford to play them for the second time this season. This is a newspaper account of that day-

"When the Hutchinson team left here early Saturday morning, the weather was warm and balmy and there was little thought that the game would be played in a fierce blizzard and snowstorm. Many of the Hutchinson boys did not take overcoats, and none of them took heavy clothing in which to play the game. The Hutchinson team never got warmed up. Their thin neckless jerseys afforded no protection against the cold blasts and the players shivered and shook and played football like a bunch of frozen snails." Source: *Hutchinson News*, November 13, 1911.

Not only did things go bad, they got worse. The referees scheduled for the game didn't show up.

"Coach Yeoman and Bailey had agreed upon some officials who have been working in Central Kansas this season. These men lived in Stafford. Duck shooting was too good to resist so they left early Saturday morning and left the two high school teams in the lurch for competent officials. Two men were secured who were entirely ignorant of the finer points of the game. They did not show a spirit of unfairness but merely a lack of knowledge." Source-*Hutchinson News*, November 11, 1911

The 'new' officials showed their lack of knowledge by allowing numerous blunders in awarding the ball on several occasions to the home team, even though Hutchinson clearly should have had possession. On one play, due to the extreme cold weather, Hutchinson only had 10 players on the field since Hiram Patten had walked off the field without telling anyone. The weather played in Stafford's favor since they were better prepared while Hutchinson was not. The entire squad was feeling downtrodden and even Butler, the star player, was ready to walk off the field. Shortly after the second Stafford touchdown, Coach Yeoman yielded to quitting, fearful for his players safety from the elements. Hutchinson lost 10-5 with the only score provided by a 60-yard touchdown run. Many times throughout the season, opposing teams would try to sit or jump on Butler's head after being tackled, all in the name of taking him out of the game.

November 18, 1911 saw the Salters get back on track with a 35-6 beating of Sterling High. A veteran Hutchinson player from the late 1890's squad commented on Hutchinson's linemen of that game, "Giles and Gleadall opened up holes through which you could drive a load of hay." The last game of the season had previously been played against the local Salt City Business College on Thanksgiving Day, but that tradition was discontinued after the 1910 season when the college dropped its football program. This year, the Salters played against the Benders from Great Bend on November 30. Hutchinson won decidedly by a score of 35-0 and finished the season with a 5-1-2 record. Butler scored 14 touchdowns for a total of 70 points in his freshman year and the Salters were determined to be the mythical state football champions of the state of Kansas.

BUTLER MAKES FINE RECORD DURING THE FOOTBALL SEASON

Played in Magnificent Form All Season—Promises to be a Star Foot Ball Player.

SALT CITY HIGHS HOLD LYONS WITHOUT A SCORE

RICE-COUNTY LADS PLAYED A ROUGH CONTEST.

Hutchinson Lads Outplayed Opponents, but Officials Differed and Penalized Unjustly— Two Negroes.

While the football men were practicing Thursday evening on the lot north of the building, someone kicked the ball out onto the road. Just then a dignified colored minister passed and oblidgingly started to get the ball for the boys. Now everyone knows how hard it is to catch a football on the bounce. Its shape makes it bound, first one way and then another. The obliging minister spread out his arms and started after the ball, and finally getting it after it came to a dead standstill. Some of the boys saw Sol Butler, the negro halfback rolling on the ground, convulsing with laughter. When asked what was the matter, Sol said, "He went after that football jest like he was tryin' to catch a chicken." November 12, 1911 The *Hutchinson Gazette*

1911 Hutchinson Football Team Back row-Coach Donald Yeoman, unknown, unknown, unknown, unknown, unknown, unknown. Middle row-unknown, unknown, unknown, Clarence Phillips, unknown, unknown, Coach Edward Daigle. Bottom row-Captain Joe Gleadall, Hiram Patten, unknown, Solomon Butler. Source- The *High School Buzz*, 1912

Winter's harshness came and went in Kansas and soon Butler's attention turned to the track and field season. The first meet occurred on April 13, 1912 as Hutchinson participated in the Stafford Dual Meet, and ended up winning the meet with 57 points, with Stafford placing second with 40 points. Butler placed first in four events: the 100-yard dash in 10.6 seconds, the 220-yard run in 25 seconds, the long jump at 19 feet, 5 ½ inches, the 220 low hurdles in 29.6 seconds. He also placed second in the shot put and third in the high jump.

The tracksters from Hutchinson then traveled to the Cooper College Invitational in Sterling, Kansas on April 20, 1912, where they won 8 of the 12 events and scored 50 points to win the meet. High schools that participated in this meet were Reno County, Sterling, Kinsley, and Leoti. Again, Butler showed his dominance by placing first in the 100-yard dash, 220, 220 low hurdles, and the long jump. On April 27, 1912, Hutchinson joined Sterling, Reno County, Great Bend, Stafford, Ellinwood, Pratt, St. John, Halstead, McPherson, Kingman, and Kinsley High Schools at the Hutchinson Fairgrounds in a pouring rainstorm for the Central Kansas Athletic Association 7th District Track meet, where again, they won the meet with 34 points to Great Bend's second place finish with 16 points. Butler won three events here: the 100-yard dash in 11 1-5 seconds, the 220 low hurdles in 31 3-5 seconds, and the long jump in 18 feet, 10 ½ inches. Hutchinson won the team championship and Butler was awarded a gold cup for the most individual points with 18.

Next on their schedule was the Kansas University Interscholastic Track Meet in Lawrence on May 4, 1912, where 300 athletes from 45 schools participated. This meet was touted as a showdown between Butler and Great Bend's Porter who was reputed to be the fastest man in western Kansas. Individually, Butler won the 50 yard dash in 5 4-5 seconds, the 100-yard dash in 10 1-5 seconds (setting the state record) the 220 low hurdles in 26 seconds, and finished third in the long jump. Hutchinson finished second with 37 1/2 points, with Butler scoring 21 of the points.

On May 10, 1912, the Salters traveled to Wichita to play at the Ark Valley Interscholastic Meet at Fairmont College, where Butler won gold medals in the 100 and 220 events. Due to an undisclosed dispute in the 220-yard dash, Butler quit the event. Hutchinson coach Yeoman left the meet, thinking it would be called off due to the downpour of rain. He left senior Ralph Pattison in charge of the team that stayed behind. Butler had entered the broad jump and the shot put, but did not compete in those events. Hutchinson finished the meet in third place with 23 points. The following week, Coach Yeoman received word from Fairmont College that Hutchinson had won the meet last week, and they would be awarded the grand prize cup.

With track season over, Butler turned his athletic efforts to baseball as he played for the high school team again.

The 1912 football season saw the Salters of Hutchinson play their first 10-game season and earned an 8-1-1 record and the Kansas State championship title. The Blue and Gold boys accumulated a total of 325 points compared to their opponents' 69 points. The first game of the season, on September 28, saw the Hutch men travel to Sterling and defeated them soundly by a score of 78-0. Butler scored seven touchdowns on this day, setting a school record that still stands to this day. Touchdowns were now awarded six points, the first year for this change. The second game of the season, the overly zealous team, riding high from last week's game, played dismally to a 0-0 tie over Stafford. Game three of the season had the Salters travel to the always dominant Wichita High team. Sadly, they returned with a 21-13 loss. The Hutchinson record in the short season was 1-1-1.

1912 H Men Football Banquet   **Sophomore Solomn Butler**

Over the stretch of the next seven games, the Hutchinson boys were able to win all of them, beating Nickerson 33-13, Kingman 38-0, Wichita 28-0, Salina 57-0, Nickerson 27-17, Pratt 13-7 and Kingman 35-3. At the end of the season, Butler had scored 31 touchdowns for a total of 186 points as a sophomore. Coach Yoeman resigned at the end of the season. Interestingly, leaders in both Topeka and Hutchinson met to plan a 'true' state football championship, but the game never materialized since it would have been played in the cold weather of December and both teams were into their respective basketball seasons, during which many of the athletes played in both sports.

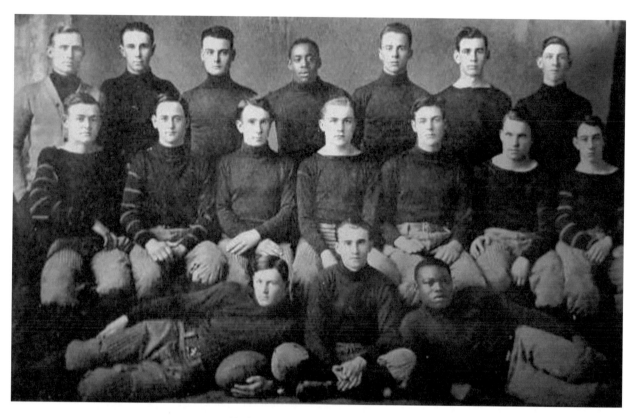

1912 Hutchinson Football Team

Back row-Coach Don Yeoman, Max Wyman, Errol McDermett, Clarence Phillips, Chester Woodson, Freese, Delbert Hawk. Middle row-William Hughes, Louis Howard, John Foster, Eldon Smith, Chauncey Yeoman, Minot English, Milford Hartman. Front row-Captain Robert Bacon, George Duckworth, Solomon Butler. Source- The *High School Annual Yearbook*

Details about several of Butler's sophomore year track events are sketchy, other than to note that he participated in the Stafford Dual Track Meet and the Wichita Dual Track Meet. At the April 26th 7th District Interscholastic Meet in Pratt, Butler and his school competed against 35 other schools, with Hutchinson winning the meet with 58 points. Butler won seven events, broke five meet records and unofficially broke the world record in the 50-yard dash. Hutchinson won the team cup, and the relay cup, and Butler won the individual cup. He placed first in the 60- yard dash with a time of 5.4 seconds, the 100-yard dash with a time of 10.3 seconds, first place in the 220 low hurdles, and first in the shot put with a toss of 40 feet, 3 inches. He also finished second in the long jump. It was later determined that he had a lane violation in the 220 lows and was disqualified.

The Kansas University Interscholastic Meet ran on May 2-3 with 45 schools and 375 athletes attending. Hutchinson scored 40 points to finish second behind Lawrence with a total of 67 points to capture first. At this meet, Butler finished first in the 50-

yard dash, the 220, and in the 220 low hurdles. He gathered second place finishes in the 50-yard dash and the shot put. During the 50, Butler tripped, falling to his knees, yet collected himself and still finished second.

A pair of student drawn comics of Solomon Butler that were published in the high school newspaper, *The Buzz*

Butler and the Hutchinson track team found themselves at the Arkansas Valley Interscholastic Meet at Fairmont College in Wichita on May 10 with Butler winning the 50-yard dash, the 220, 220 low hurdles, and the long jump. He also finished second in the 100-yard dash with a time of 10.6 seconds and in the shot put. The following week was another stellar week at the Kansas State Agricultural College State Interscholastic Meet in Manhattan, as Butler again collected 21 points to claim the individual cup. In the 100-yard dash, Hardy of Kansas City finished first, Butler finishing second, and Wright from Lawrence High rounding out third place. Butler finished first in the 50, 220, 220 lows, and the shot put. He also finished second in the 100, the long jump, and the mile relay. He went on to set 5 meet records in his events. The *Topeka Daily Capitol* newspaper sponsored the individual cup, but unfortunately, Butler never received it. Hutchinson High School won the Kansas State Track Championship.

Not only was Butler a gifted athlete, he loved to entertain and make people laugh as seen in this advertisement in the May 24, 1913 edition of the *Hutchinson Gazette*.

The 1913 Hutchinson High School track team

Again, in the summer of 1913, Butler played baseball for the Gold and Blue.

The fall of 1913 saw a few changes at Hutchinson High with the hiring of Herbert N. Roe as the head football coach. Roe graduated from the University of California and Colorado University, and taught English and coached football, basketball, and track. Although Roe was only at Hutchinson for one year, he was highly respected for his work ethic and for how he handled what was to become a controversial football season.

October 4 was the first game of the 1913 season against St. John High School, and the Salters beat the home team 44-20, with Butler scoring three touchdowns. The following week, at a home game with over 3,000 fans in attendance, Hutchinson beat Salina 15-7, and Butler scored two touchdowns. The rivalry with Stafford continued on October 25, with the home Blue and Gold pounding the visitors 41-0. Again, Butler scored an impressive five touchdowns. On November 1, the boys from Hutchinson played against a group of soldiers from Fort Riley, at a game originally scheduled with Lawrence High. The reason for this change was that the Lawrence

High officials made it very clear that they were drawing "the color line" and would not play against a school that allowed black athletes to participate. This was somewhat hypocritical, since in the years prior to 1913, Lawrence touted black players on its rosters. The principal at Hutchinson, S.L. Palmer, contacted the officials in Lawrence that Hutchinson still wanted to play and even offered the rival school 50 percent of the game revenue. Coach Roe and Principal Palmer stood their ground by stating they would not play without Butler and Phillips, the two black players in question. Lawrence stood fast in its decision not to play the game, so Palmer had to fill the vacancy left by the uncooperative team. Hutchinson went on to defeat the Fort Riley soldiers 27-6, with Butler nursing a sprained shoulder. He scored two touchdowns and had two interceptions.

The team from Emporia traveled to Hutchinson on November 7, only to be soundly drubbed by a score of 55-10. Again, Butler scored three touchdowns. The Salters traveled to Kingman on November 14 and defeated them 35-3. Their only loss of the season came at the hands of Marion, who won 34-19, largely because several Hutchinson players were hospitalized due to illness. This date was originally scheduled to play against Great Bend High, but because six of its players had been suspended for post-game conduct, Hutchinson would have had to play the junior varsity team. Principal Palmer thought it best not to play against the lesser-experienced boys, and then scheduled the team from Marion.

A former player from Great Bend recalled years after a game against Butler that, "I didn't like Negroes and decided I'd get Butler." He attempted to spear Butler and, "the next thing I knew I was being carried out with a broken collarbone. I thought I'd been hit by a locomotive."

Butler and this player ended up shaking hands after the game in a mutual display of good sportsmanship.

The student body of Hutchinson High in 1913. Source-Steve Miller

Butler carries the ball around the right end as a junior at Hutchinson.

Again, the "color line" was laid out by the school officials from Pratt High as the parents of two of their best players stated that "they could not stand to play against a 'negro' boy." And again, Coach Roe and Principal Palmer held firm that their two black players would play and not be benched. The game was cancelled and Palmer, again, found a replacement team with Nickerson High coming to Hutchinson and losing 46-6. Butler scores three touchdowns in the win. The final game of the year saw the Salters road trip to Salina, only to defeat the Mustangs 34-12 with Butler scoring four touchdowns.

The Salters finished the season with an 8-1 record and another Kansas State Championship title. Butler stated this was the best Hutchinson team on which he had played. He finished the year with 23 touchdowns and 146 points to his credit. In all, Butler scored a career 66 touchdowns and 404 points as a left halfback at Hutchinson High School, and had received six varsity letters in football, baseball, and track.

The hypocrisy of the season lay in the fact that Lawrence had earlier in the year played Baldwin High, with a black player on its roster, as did Peabody High when Pratt played against them. It was quite apparent that the coaches of these schools did not want their players being upstaged by the black players named Solomon Butler and Clarence Phillips.

1913 Hutchinson football team

Back row: Earl Knieper, Solomon Butler, George Nichols, Leonard Clinton, Chauncey Yeoman, Ellis Ellsworth, Clarence Phillips, Coach Roe. Front row-Johnny Armstrong, John Foster, Eldon Smith, Captain Minot English, Gerald Rexroad, Lyman.

The bitter cold evening of February 13, 1914 didn't deter the Hutchinson football team from presenting a minstrel performance at the high school, with all of the players performing a song or dance. Butler and Clarence Phillips brought the house down with their clog dancing routine. Coach Roe also got into the act and did some songs and dancing, much to the delight of the 250 students and local citizens who attended the event.

The Rock Island Lines depot in Hutchinson where Sol departed to participate at the Northwestern University Interscholastic Indoor Meet in 1914 and eventually relocate to Rock Island, Illinois.

The head track coach of Kansas University, W. O. Hamilton, was aware that Butler was an outstanding track athlete, but would not recruit him due to his skin color. Hamilton did, however, contact Northwestern University's track coach Lewis Omer about Butler's achievements in high school track. Omer in turn, wrote a letter to the new Hutchinson High coach, Herbert Roe, inviting Butler to participate at the Northwestern Interscholastic Indoor Track Meet on March 27, 1914, in Evanston, Illinois. Local businessmen in Hutchinson, with the support and permission of Coach Roe, raised money to assist fundraising efforts to send Butler to the Chicago area to compete in this exclusive meet. Butler traveled by train, along with his brother Ben, to the event.

Lewis Omer, NU Coach

Patten Gymnasium on the Northwestern campus

On March 27-28, 1914, Butler competed at his very first large-scale indoor meet, facing over 300 of the finest athletes from all over the Midwest. Competing as the sole representative from Hutchinson, Kansas High School had to be a very unsettling feeling, with no teammates for support. However, this did not factor into what would soon be a historic sporting moment. Butler won the individual cup for the most points scored by one athlete, and his solo performance garnered a fourth-place finish overall. He won the 60-yard dash preliminary with a time of 6.25 seconds, setting the high school interscholastic world record. He also set a conference record in the 60-yard high hurdles with a time of 8.15 seconds. When the finals were run on the 28th, Butler placed first in the 60-yard dash with a world record time of 6.2 seconds, and a world record in the 60-yard low hurdles with a time of 8 seconds. He also won the long jump with a leap of 20 feet, 8 ½ inches, and finished second in the 440 and the shot put. Northwestern University's coach called Butler "the greatest athlete west of Chicago, either amateur or professional." When word reached Butler's father about his accomplishments, his dad made the following statement, "He equaled the world's record in that sixty-yard dash and he done broke the broad jump record and if he'd just take a little more pains, and not knocked down hurdles, he'd have won second place." He continued on, "But he's goin' to tear Chicago wide open when he goes up there in June. And at Pratt, why man, he's going t' bring back all the cups they got to Hutchinson." The elder Butler, obviously very proud, also said with confidence, "And let me tell you somethin', My boy'll be runnin' that hundred in 5 seconds after a few risin's and settin's of the sun. And the beauty about it all is, Sol ain't swelled up over what he does. He never says a word to nobody when he wins them races. He's just happy to be able to win points for high school. He never tells me about it."

BUTLER A SENSATION IN NORTHWESTERN MEET

NEGRO BOY FEATURED IN ALL CHICAGO PAPERS.

Sol Broke One Northwestern Record and Tied a World's Mark— Pratt Got a Fourth.

Not only did his dad notice, the world took notice.

Solomon Butler and his brother Ben returned from Chicago to Hutchinson on March 31, and were met at the Rock Island Lines depot at 6:30 a.m. by their father, friend and fellow teammate Clarence Phillips, and police officer Bill Owens. Owens provided the Butler brothers and their entourage a ride to the family home on West Avenue B where he was received by the family. After a brief rest, he was greeted at 10:30 a.m. by a large group of friends, members of the church, and other members of the local black community. Riding in a large touring car, the hometown hero was escorted by the police and a black band to the high school. Here, Butler was met by his track team, fellow students, and a host of Hutchinson citizens to wish him congratulations for his accomplishments in Chicago. During the parade, handbills were distributed to the crowd announcing the celebration that evening.

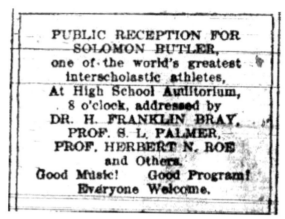

PUBLIC RECEPTION FOR
SOLOMON BUTLER,
one of the world's greatest
interscholastic athletes,
At High School Auditorium,
8 o'clock, addressed by
DR. H. FRANKLIN BRAY,
PROF. S. L. PALMER,
PROF. HERBERT N. ROE
and Others.
Good Music!   Good Program!
Everyone Welcome.

This was a surprise to Principal Palmer, since no one had asked him about it. He obviously conceded and participated.

Later in the evening, a reception was attended by over 200 people, and accolades were given by his minister, Dr. H. Franklin Bray, Solomon's father Benjamin, Principal S.L. Palmer and Coach Herbert Roe.

After returning from Evanston, a letter to the editor to the *Daily Northwestern* was published on April 3, 1914, from a prominent lawyer John H. Wigmore, spelling out details of Butler's visit.

"It is a pitiful thing to see a child stunted and maimed by the inherited vices and weaknesses of its parents—defects which it had no part in making or meriting. And it is depressing to see young men perpetuate by mere imitation the unfounded prejudices of an older generation and a distant community. And this sad spectacle becomes more discouraging when these young men's own fathers were the very ones who fought their lives away to stamp out these prejudices and meannesses. Last week, an athlete from Kansas was to come here to the meet. The fraternities had drawn for the allotment of the various guests. When this particular athlete came, he happened to go directly to the gymnasium, where he met first the head coach, an officer of the University. This officer discovered that the expected athlete was colored, instead of white. Believing with reason that the students to whose hospitality the visitor had been allotted would refuse to receive a colored student like a white student, he allotted him to a public house of entertainment kept for hire by a colored man. This was carried out. And so the young gentlemen of the fraternity were spared the association with a colored brother student. Since that time, and to avoid a similar mischance, the allotment for guests at the interscholastic meet stipulated in advance that no colored student visitor should be placed in the university quarters with our white students. It is not my purpose to criticize the action of the University officer. It is my purpose to call attention to the facts. Here are groups of young men living in a land which bled its best blood for equal treatment of white and black—studying the ideals of all the past ages—aiming to be self-respecting

gentlemen—cultivating the bravest and the highest principles of humanity—acknowledging the religious faith which proclaims all mankind as brethren. And yet they start out in life with practicing the most pitiful kind of snobbery—the snobbery of color. And they have the excuse of the South. The South inherited its troubles—inherited them from the misguided ancestors who robbed the black man from his house and made him a slave. I have no desire to quarrel here with the South and with what its people do on their own soil. But here, on Northern soil, there is no such inheritance. To oust the colored man from equal treatment here is merely an acquired snobbery, and the more inexcusable. Those of you who have not reflected on it should send to the Juvenile Protective Association of Chicago for its recent pamphlet on "The Colored People of Chicago." In it you will read how the increasing snobbery of race—snobbery of the sons of twenty five races of immigrants from all parts of Europe, has rapidly increased of late years, and it is driving the colored people out of decent gainful employments—driving them out of all opportunities to live decently. And you will read that almost the only remaining places where the line is not drawn are the universities. The universities? Had the author of that pamphlet but known, even this distinguished position could not have been accorded to them. Put yourself for a moment in the position of a well-bred university student, of colored skin, who is receiving such treatment from his fellow students, and look forward with him the prospects of his career in life. And then ask yourself if this would seem a world of reason and justice. Of the young men and women who read this I ask: Face the question squarely and soberly now-now, while your ideals are powerful and your motives unmixed. Face it as a question of conscience. Take down your Lowell, your Longfellow, your Emerson, your Lincoln, your Whittier, your Bible—take all the high things you believe in, and marshal them before your unprejudiced self. Ask that self whether you can reconcile with those high things that you believe in the open and absolute refusal to treat equally a colored student simply because of his or her color. If you cannot reconcile it, then either give up professing those high principles, or give up this treatment. A frank, cruel aristocracy of color would be a more wholesome thing than an inconsistent snobbery. Signed John H. Wigmore"

A major highlight of Butler's high school career was receiving a letter from Lewis Omer, director of athletics at Northwestern University. The letter reads-

Mr. Solomon Butler,

My Dear Sir:--

I am making a special point trophy for you, which will not be finished for a few days. It is a shield instead of a cup, and I think will be a better looking trophy; will remain nicer longer than a cup would. I will send it to you as soon as it is finished.

I want you to be sure and come up to Stagg's meet and stay at Northwestern, as there is a fellow from Iowa who is supposed to be a much better man than anyone in the country. I am sure that you can beat him. He has never shown better than 10 flat, but thinks he is unbeatable. If you come to Northwestern I will see that you get on the Olympic team, if I have to raise the money by subscription to send you to Berlin. I am sure that if you will take care of yourself and be careful of the way in which you live, you will qualify without a doubt.

Sincerely yours,

LEWIS OMER, Director of Athletics

Butler's high school track career continued on April 26 at the 7th District Meet in Pratt. Here, the Hutchinson tracksters won the meet with a total of 42 points, with Butler gathering 30 of the points himself, placing first in the following events- 50-yard dash in 5.25 seconds (setting a high school interscholastic world record), the 100-yard dash in 9.45 seconds (another world record), the 220 in 22.5 seconds, the 220 low hurdles in 25 1-5 seconds, the broad jump with a leap of 22 feet, 1 inch, and the shot put with a throw of 44 feet, 2 1/2 inches. The weather was ideal and the grandstands were packed with spectators. The co-eds from Fairmount College served the athletes lunch and presented the winners with beautiful, handmade pennants.

Sol finishing the 220-yard dash at a Kansas track meet

The following week, the Hutchinson track team traveled to the Kansas University Interscholastic Track Meet where over 300 athletes from three classes from 40 high schools competed. A steady rain fell during the day and no records were broken. Here, Butler won eight events—50-yard dash, 100-yard dash, 440, 220 high hurdles, 220 low hurdles, high jump, long jump, and the anchor in the mile relay. After the meet, he gave an impressive speech. Here is an account of that day from John C. Grover, a reporter for the *Kansas City Star* in an article dated October 11, 1931.

"In the more than a quarter of century in which I have been a patron of track and field sports as an athlete, a spectator or a starter, the most notable single man performance that has come under my observation was the work of a Negro boy. A Negro boy in high school.

And of all the speeches I have heard at athletic dinners the brief talk of this Negro boy that night has left the most lasting impression.

It was an afternoon in Lawrence in 1914. Hamilton had re-established the interscholastic meet at Kansas and the athletes of the state high schools were displaying their prowess on the old McCook field.

The Negro boy who is the hero of this story was there as a representative of the Hutchinson high school. In the trials of the 50-yard dash he won each trial heat he was in and captured the final. He breezed through the trial heats of the 100-yard dash, winning each and then adding to his laurels victory in the century finals.

And then the Hurdles

In the 220-yard heats he won each and then the final. He won the 440-yard dash and then he was first in the running broad jump with a flying leap of nearly 22 feet. Last he was an entry in the low hurdles.

The boys had been called to their marks when this Negro boy turned to me. "Boss," he said after lifting his hand as we used to do in the public schools when seeking permission to ask a question, "May I speak to my coach?" I gave consent and overheard the boy's conversation with his high school principal who also was his coach. "How shall I run this race, coach?" he asked, "Just set a good fast pace and keep it?" "That's the way," said the principal-coach.

Obviously, this Negro lad never had run the hurdles. Over the first hurdle he leaped like a broad jumper, both feet together and in front of him. Over the second hurdle he used high jumping form, turning sideways, putting one leg over then the other in scissors style. He evidently had figured between hurdles that the first method was impracticable.

And so, alternating between these two styles, with modifications and variations he topped each of the next ten hurdles and at the finish the boy was a hurdle and a half ahead of the field.

When the spoils of the afternoon had been distributed among victors this Negro boy from Hutchinson wore eight medals for first place victories. He had run the last lap of the relay race which his team won and mainly through his individual efforts the Hutchinson high had finished first in the meet.

Guest at a Huge Dinner

That night, the University of Kansas gave a great banquet to the visiting athletes and their coaches. There were five or six hundred visitors, not more than four or five of them Negro boys; all the others white. There were 1,000 persons at that dinner.

Before the evening was over, the Negro lad of this story was called on to say a few words. It was a delicate situation. I wondered how the boy would meet the test. Would he be boastful or modest? Would he boast a bit over his remarkable string of victories or would he minimize his efforts?

The Negro boy arose and I quote him word for word.

"My coach has taught me three things," he said, "first, my God; second, my country; third, my school. Today I did the best I could for my school."

He sat down, a thunderous applause ringing in his ears. He had met the situation gloriously, topping his wonderful work of the day by as fine and unaffected a speech as any athlete ever made.

Sol Butler was the name of this Negro boy from Hutchinson as you probably have guessed. Later he represented the United States in the Olympic Games and his reputation as a remarkable athlete and a fine sportsman was coast to coast wide.

(Author's note—Apparently Mr. Grover recalled a few of these facts incorrectly, since Butler had just set a world record in the 60-yard hurdles at Northwestern)

This trophy was awarded to the Hutchinson High School track team on May 2, 1914. Source-Paul Waggoner collection

Six days later, the Salters traveled to Wichita to compete at the Arkansas Valley Interscholastic Meet, held at Fairmont College. Thirty-five schools competed at the meet with over 250 athletes participating; with Hutchinson winning the Class A title with 48 points for the third consecutive year. Once again, Butler garnered the individual point trophy and placed first in five events—100-yard dash in 10 seconds, 220 in 22.4 seconds, the 120 low hurdles in 14 seconds, long jump in 21 feet, 6 inches, the shot put at 43 feet, 6 inches, and placed fourth in the discus. For an unknown reason, this meet did not include the 50-yard dash or the 220 low hurdles. Butler gave a wonderful speech at the state meet banquet held after the event.

Butler and the remainder of the Hutchinson track team returned to Evanston, Illinois on June 13 for the Northwestern University Invitational Outdoor Meet at the invite of Alonzo Stagg, the meet director. Once again, community leaders and friends raised funds to send the team to travel to this event, and his brother Ben accompanied him. Butler arrived a week before the start of the meet to work out with the Northwestern coach, Lewis Omer. Over 500 athletes from 90 high schools attended this premier event. Once again, Butler won the individual points honor. The man to beat at this meet was a fast sprinter named Carter, who hailed from Chicago University High School. Butler bested him in the 100-yard dash with a time of 10 seconds; but placed second to Carter in the 220. Butler finished second in the 220 low hurdles and first in the long jump with a major leap of 21 feet, 11 ½ inches, which also set a meet record. This jump placed him one foot and 11 ½ inches ahead of the second-place finisher. Butler also established a world record in the 60-yard dash, and a high school interscholastic record in the 60-yard dash preliminaries. Hutchinson gathered enough points to finish in second place out of the 99 schools entered, quite an impressive feat. After the meet, Butler was asked to say a few words about his school and the team. Alonzo Stagg proclaimed that "Solomon Butler was the fastest athlete west of the Mississippi." After the meet, Butler and his brother Ben were invited to stay in Chicago for several weeks while Coach Roe worked with John R. Richards, Superintendent of Sports and Playgrounds in the parks of southern Chicago.

While in Chicago, Butler was asked to participate in a Chicago Athletic Club meet in Grant Park and would face one of the finest runners in the country, Joe Loomis. In the 120-yard dash, Butler finished just inches behind Loomis in a near photo-finish. Butler enjoyed running against Loomis and had hoped to compete against him in a future race, which he did. Butler also participated in several other meets in the area during the summer and realized that there was no "color line," he was being accepted for his exceptional talent. It was at this time that he began to think about relocating to a bigger high school, somewhere in the Midwest, where the competition would be more comparable to his own skills. Rumors abounded that Butler would attend Evanston High School because of his relationship with Northwestern University's Coach Omer. That never materialized. Butler would give this explanation for his move to Rock Island.

"When I began to see the exceptional chances for an athlete in Illinois, I decided that I would attend school somewhere in the state the following year. About this time my coach, Mr. H. N. Roe, accepted a position as director of athletics in the schools of Rock Island. I soon afterward asked my coach if he would care if I wrote the superintendent there to see if there was a good chance for me to help pay my way, and if my brother Ben would have a chance. Both Mr. Roe and Mr. Coach Roe, as he had developed me and gave me a chance to compete in higher athletics. A good many people wonder why I came to Rock Island to attend school. It was simply a case of deep gratitude and friendship I feel for Mr. Roe and the desire to stay with him, together with my plan for running in the bigger meets in the Middle West. I could have gone to many other schools and, perhaps, have gotten along better, but I picked Rock Island for the reasons I have mentioned.'

--Solomon Butler, "Three Years in High School Athletics

Before leaving Hutchinson, Butler looked back in retrospect on what could help the track team become better. *"When I first entered his High School, some three and one half years ago, I thought this building was the biggest and grandest school building I had ever seen. As a matter of fact it was. As I went from class room to class room, on that first day, I became more and more impressed with the fine modern equipment I saw everywhere. Finally, as the day drew to a close, I passed by the big bulletin board, on the second floor, and saw written in large white letters, 'This is the seventh period.' I glanced at my schedule card and saw the word, 'Gymnasium,' written there after the figure. Upon my application, a good natured upperclassman, who happened to be standing near, directed me to the gym and, as rapidly as my feet would carry me, I scampered to my destination. Upon reaching the gym I thought, 'My! This is the greatest place in all this grand building.' After our instructor had called the roll, he told us that we could go up in the balcony and run around it for our exercise that first day. After the first few laps I discovered that it was exceedingly bothersome and tiresome to slow down each time we had to go around those 'square corners.' I thought it was a shame that it was not better arranged and I wondered if all gyms arranged so poorly. Before my freshman year was over I discovered another smaller school whose gym was much better arranged than ours. It was during the basketball season and Hutchinson High School was scheduled to play Reno County High School in Nickerson. A large crowd of rooters were going with the team and I planned to go along. Upon entering the Nickerson gym I immediately noticed, first, that is was much larger than ours. Second, instead of having square corners in had round corners. Finally, in place of our little narrow balcony, their gym had a regular running track, with slanted sides. Above the running track was a balcony fully as large, if not larger than ours, and consequently just as able to accommodate their basketball crowds. It occurred to me then and I have felt the same way since, that if Nickerson High School could afford a gym with a running track like that, that certainly Hutchinson High School ought to be able to afford one equally as good."*

Butler would soon find out that when he arrived at Rock Island High School, they had a much smaller gym than Hutchinson did, with no balcony to run on. The new Rock Island YMCA, just a block away from the high school, would have just what Butler needed.

The Rock Island YMCA was brand new when Butler moved to Rock Island.

BETHEL A. M. E. CHURCH
REV H. FRANKLIN GRAY, D. D., PASTOR

I helped build this church for the colored people of Hutchinson, Kansas.

This is the church Sol attended as a boy and later when visiting his parents.

HUTCHINSON WON MEET

Made 43 Points in Arkansas Valley Interscholastic Events.

SOL BUTLER WAS A STAR

Black Athlete Took Five Firsts and One Fourth Yesterday.

UNIVERSITY HIGH TAKES PREP MEET OVER 115 SCHOOLS

Carter, Spink, and Shiverick Give Locals Honors in Stagg Field Games.

BUTLER OF KANSAS LEADER

Colored Star Puts Hutchinson School in Second Place; Rain Prevents Broken Records.

THE TRACK TEAM

Carl Donnell.   Theron Brown.   Herbert N. Roe, Coach.   Chester Bates.   George Booher.
            Reid Freese.   Darwin Pattinson. Captain.   Sol Butler.

1914 Hutchinson High School track team   Source- Steve Miller

Chapter 3-
The senior year at Rock Island

Rock Island Senior High School where Butler attended his senior year. Source- Rock Island County Historical Society

In July of 1914, Mr. Herbert N. Roe accepted the position of athletic director and football and track coach at Rock Island, Illinois High School, along the banks of the Mississippi River. Butler and his brother Ben, transferred to Rock Island High School and eventually moved in with Coach Roe at 502-23rd Street. Butler sent a letter to the Hutchinson newspaper to clarify his reasons on moving from Kansas to Rock Island. Understandably, the citizens of Hutchinson were extremely shocked and disappointed that they had lost Butler. In a *Daily Dispatch* interview on September 28, 1914, he explained his reasons for moving to Rock Island, after reading in the Hutchinson, Kansas newspaper of their displeasure with him.

"I was reading an article in your paper wherein it stated that I was persuaded by Coach Herbert N. Roe to attend the high school at Rock Island. I wish to correct that statement. The reason I am now attending Rock Island is, first, because I stand a better chance, two to one, to get into all the big meets between Chicago and Kansas City.

"The locality is better here for athletics, the people are more enthusiastic, and they judge a man only by his ability and by his gentlemanly qualities.

"Second I would very much like to attend high school at home, but you know that a lot of towns around there refused to play Hutchinson on account of my being on the team, and as I didn't want to cause any hard feelings, and neither discontinue my athletic career, I thought it best that I should change schools.

"The third reason that I am at Rock Island is that I owe a deep debt of gratitude to Coach Roe for giving me the chance to compete in eastern athletics, and as Mr. Roe and I are the very best of friends, and as I was either going to Evanston, or some other school I picked Rock Island because Coach Roe was there and I didn't think I could be mistaken in continuing my training under him."

Moline Dispatch interview with Butler about leaving Kansas

It was extremely obvious that Ben Butler Sr. was proud of his son. A reporter once asked him about his son's upcoming meets in Rock Island and in Chicago, and he said, "I told my boy, Sol, to only hit the ground twice in that race Saturday. If they crowd him, that boy Solomon will sure do that hundred in nine flat. He'll sure hit one place in the middle and then the tape. Ain't nothing going to pass him but the wind, that's sure." He loved to tell of his son's exploits at his business establishment, located on the corner of Avenue B and Main, a shoe shine stand and a pop stand that sold an ice cold concoction called "Strawberry Finish."

A poem written by a Hutchinson High student in the October 16, 1914 school newspaper after losing Butler to Rock Island High School.

THE CRY OF H.H.S.

Alone, upon the prairies to the west,

I stand and watch the threatening in the sky;

The threatening of my death writ in the west;

Come back to me, Sol Butler, or I die!

Before my feet the football ground is laid;

Before my feet the enemies teams here lie;

And I am here, the victim of their raid;

Come back to me, Sol Butler, or I die!

My football team is young and lacks in skill;

Conquered by Kingsman's football team team am I;

Feeble and weak, she bent me to her will,

Come back to me, Sol Butler, ere I die!

Solomon and his brother Ben lived in this house with Coach Roe.   Source- City of Rock Island

Butler and his brother Ben arrived on the 9:15 p.m. train from Hutchinson, Kansas on September 8, 1914, and were enrolled at Rock Island High School the following day. Butler immediately joined the football team. Practices were conducted daily at Reservoir Park, a nine-block trek up 22nd Street hill from the high school on 7th Avenue and 21nd Street.   During a practice on Sept 12, William Whisler was returning a punt when Butler made a flying tackle on him, splitting Whisler's lip open and twisting his leg, causing him to miss the next day of practice. The first game of the season at Rock Island was set aside as an alumni game, with the current team beating the alums 7-0 on September 27. A large turnout of over 1,000 fans came to Island City Park at 3:10 p.m. to witness the legendary Butler and the highly touted eleven led by the new coach. Roe stated that he would consider the game a defeat if his team could not run up more than 25 points against the graduates. However, over half of the players on the alumni team were current Rock Island Independents players, a professional team also based at Island City Park. Butler would start at left halfback, and an errant whistle called back a touchdown scored by Butler. A crowd of 100 Davenport fans attended the game to 'spy' on the legendary Butler to see what they would be facing in the near future. An unfortunate incident occurred during the alumni game as Butler was on a long end run and was forced out of bounds and made contact with a young boy, August Lutz, who was watching the game on the sidelines. Lutz was carried to the grandstands where he was placed in an ambulance and attended to by Dr. C. F. Freytag at the boys' home. The boy incurred a fracture on the right leg above the knee. Butler had multiple runs of 50 and 40 yards, and finished the game with well over 200 yards rushing, and after the game, went to check on the little injured boy.

Week two of the season had the always fast Aledo, Illinois team visit Rock Island for a 3:10 p.m. game at Island City Park. The last time these two teams met was in 1912, when the Aledo team defeated Rock Island 6-0. Due to the popularity of the team this year, a special streetcar was hired from the Tri-City Railway Company to transport the team and the high school band to the stadium. The band, a new feature of the high school, and led by John W. Casto, played on the car as it traveled through downtown Rock Island.

Island City Park as it appeared when Butler played here for Rock Island High School. Source- *Rock Island Argus*

Downtown Rock Island in 1914

"A one hundred percent improvement over the last game" was stated by Coach Roe as the Rock Island eleven soundly defeated the Aledo team 76-0 on October 4. The first score of the game came on a run by Butler, but it was called back by an offside penalty. After a few more plays, Butler scored, and the extra point was missed. Rock Island kicked off to Aledo, held them on downs, and then Aledo punted to Butler, who scooped up the ball and scored again. The extra point was made this time. The second quarter began with two quick Rock Island penalties, but after this Butler scored again. In the third quarter, a play occurred that had never been seen before in local sports. Butler kicked off to Aledo, and the ball bounced off the chest of an Aledo player, bounded back to Butler in midair, who then snaked his way through the entire Aledo team and scored again, all in 18 seconds. In the fourth quarter, Butler picked off a forward pass and returned the ball for an 80-yard touchdown. At the end of the game, Butler had scored eight touchdowns (*a record that still stands today at Rock Island High School*). Roe commended the players for their great play on offense and defense, even though they had made nearly 70 yards in penalties and allowed many of the non-starters to show their skills during the game. Again, Butler rushed for over 200 yards and had over 100 yards receiving.

On October 11, 1914, the Crimson and Gold squad traveled to Rockford to face a squad that was comparable in size to a college team. In the first quarter, Rock Island held their own against the larger Rockford men, yet the lack of a good kicking game helped doom the Rocky players. That Butler punted for only 15 to 20 yards added to Rockford's advantage. Putnam and Daley, four-year starting linemen for Rockford, opened large holes in Rock Island's line, which helped Rockford score. Rock Island's offense made passes of 30 and 40 yards; but was unable to capitalize on them. Those attending the game highly praised Butler's defensive plays, as he was in on every tackle, and Rock Island held Rockford to no completed forward passes. Representatives from the University of Chicago and Northwestern University were on hand to watch Butler. In the end, the Rockford team defeated the Rock Island eleven, 14-0.

Ottawa came to face Rock Island on a rainy Saturday afternoon of October 18, 1914 at Island City Park. After the defeat at Rockford, Coach Roe had drilled the Islanders severely to prepare them for this game, and it showed. In this game, Butler started at quarterback and showed exceptional skill at calling plays. In the first quarter, Rock Island had the ball on the 15-yard line on fourth down, Butler called a shift in formation and completed a dazzling double pass on which team captain Arthur Hinkley scored. Butler scored two touchdowns during the game, which was marred by numerous fumbles on both sides. Due to the bad weather conditions, a small crowd of only 400 fans attended, but they were treated to excellent music selections during the game. The second half of the game lasted only 10 minutes after both teams agreed the game would be called at 4:30 p.m. The final touchdown came at 4:29 p.m. with Butler scoring on a 50-yard interception. An Ottawa lineman was heard to say, "Here he comes, there he goes." When the score reached 53-0, the visitors agreed that the game was 'over' and wanted to catch an early train back to Ottawa.

Monmouth High School's coach, Mr. Carlson, had scouted Butler at the Ottawa game and was quoted, *"The Rock Island bunch is one of the best teams in this section of the state, so Monmouth will have to go some to hold its own. The mainstay of the Rock Island eleven is "Sol" Butler, from Hutchinson, Kansas. Anyone who followed the results of Coach Stagg's invitation to meet for the past two years knows Sol as a colored fellow who is as fast as lightning, being a 10-second man in the century dash, and in football togs, he is a demon. The Monmouth pigskin fans look to this game as the biggest game of the year for them. They will admit that it will be the hardest one yet to be played by their eleven."*

The Islander high school team visited Augustana College to play the college's sophomore team for a practice game on October 21, with Rock Island tying the college boys 13-13. Butler played quarterback and scored both touchdowns for the high schoolers.

Coach Roe's scoring machine showed up again on October 25 at Island City Park as the home team thrashed the visiting Monmouth team, 73-0. The first quarter of the game, both teams played to a standstill, with Monmouth putting up a good fight. During the second quarter, Hinkley was pulled from the game due to an injury, and backup Vivian Thomas filled in admirably and made many outstanding running plays. Roe did not start Butler at quarterback for this game and it was evident that things just weren't clicking. Eventually, Butler was inserted in the game after numerous fumbles occurred, and he showed excellent judgment in running the team. Throughout the young season, the Islanders kicking game lacked a consistency until tackle Will Gleason was given the opportunity and made six successive goals. All of Rock Island's players performed well, including the second stringers who were given a chance to show their worth. Butler scored three touchdowns in this victory.

Rock Island played their home games at Douglas Park, and Butler would play here again in the NFL with the Rock Island Independents. Source- *Watch Tower* yearbook

In preparation for the upcoming game at Princeton on October 30 and, more importantly, the upcoming November 7th game versus Davenport, Coach Roe had very relaxed practices so that no one would get injured and to allow those who had been injured to heal. Practices were conducted behind closed doors since many 'sight-seers' from Davenport and Moline had been watching the Islanders practice; and reported back to their respective schools "the wonderful playing of Sol Butler, the local's colored demon".

Coach Roe decided to mix things up a bit for the Princeton game, sending 18 players and giving the new men a chance of playing. The Islanders boarded the train at the depot on 20th Street and steamed to Princeton, 64 miles to the east. Games against Princeton in the past had not been easy for Rock Island, even though the Crimson eleven had defeated them for the past two straight years. For this game, Roe did not attend and left the coaching duties to his assistant Keith Dooley. Dooley's boys found the Princeton team to be unexpectedly quick and formidable, having lost only one game so far this season. Princeton scored quickly in the first quarter, but as soon as Princeton kicked off to Rock Island, Butler gathered up the ball and ran through the entire Princeton defense to score. Many of the Princeton fans cheered Butler throughout the game for his stellar play. The first quarter ended at 7-7. The second quarter began with both teams exchanged punts after being held for downs, then Ackley received a pass from Butler and rambled 80 yards down the field for a touchdown. Just before the half ended, Butler intercepted a pass and ran 40 yards for a touchdown. The score at the half was 21-7. The third quarter was another exchange of punts, with neither team producing much when they had possession of the ball. The final score of the game came when Butler gathered up a Princeton punt on the 35-yard line and dashed in for another score. Rock Island had defeated Princeton for a third straight year, 27-7.

Rock Island's football team traveled by railroad to many of their away games. Source- Wilton Historical Society

Rock Island's 1914 football team pose in front of the high school. Source- *Watch Tower* yearbook

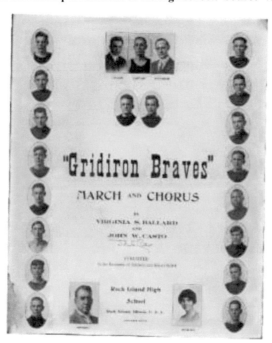

Music written by history teacher John Casto for the 1914 football team   Source- David Sebben

November 7, 1914 was a day many citizens in the Tri-City area were looking forward to. It had been seven years since Davenport High had played Rock Island in football. An unfortunate death of the Davenport High coach's son after the game, although unrelated to the game, led to the postponement of games until now. Over 300 people packed the high school auditorium a few days before the big game to relive memories of past games, practice cheers, and listen to music provided by the band. Will Griffiths, a former end and the chairman of this event, called on Arthur Mosenfelder, captain of the first team to beat Davenport in 1903, to speak of the fighting qualities of the across-the-river squad. He encouraged Rock Island's current team to play hard from whistle to whistle. Other players from the 1903 team spoke, as did Coach Roe, Principal A. J. Burton, Superintendent E. C. Fisher, Solomon Butler, and other local dignitaries.

To avoid the curious fans, Coach Roe secretly moved the practice from Island City Park to the back lot behind Horace Mann Elementary School on 14th Avenue while Coach Anderson from Augustana College marched his team up 38th Street to give Roe's players a formidable practice opponent.

The 1914 Augustana sophomore football that practiced against Rock Island at Horace Mann School. Source-Augustana College Library

This was the theme in 1914 against Davenport High, after the seven-year hiatus from playing all sports against Davenport. Source- David Sebben

Islanders Play Davenport Saturday for First Time in Seven Years

Rock Island High School Players Are Out-weighed by Davenport 13 Pounds to Man

ROCK ISLAND HIGH SCHOOL				DAVENPORT HIGH SCHOOL.			
Position—	Age	W'ght	Years				Exp in
Looby, L E	18	142	2	Position—	Age	W'ght	Years
Gleason, L T	18	163	2	Fort, R E	17	147	3
Nichols, L G	18	147	1	Koch, R T	17	150	1
Culley, C	17	144	1	Claypool, R G	18	150	1
James, R G	18	151	1	Thomson, Capt., C	20	208	3
Criswell, R T	20	151	3	Block, L G	18	160	1
Gaetjer, R E	17	160	2	Kaufmann, L T	18	180	2
Butler, Q B	19	162	3	Von Maur, L E	18	145	1
Hinkley, Capt, LH	19	146	3	Kelly, Q B	18	151	2
Ackley, R H	17	141	3	Tomson, L H	18	140	2
Whisler, F B	19	164	2	King, R H	18	180	2
				Shuler, F B	18	170	1
Average	18	152	2.01	Average	18	165	1.72
Average of Backfield		153		Average of Backfield		160	
Average of Line		151		Average of Line		174	

THE ILLINOIS HIGH SCHOOL ATHLETIC ASSOCIATION

1914-15

Names and Records of Contestants Representing _____ High School

THE PASSING MARK IN OUR HIGH SCHOOL IS

No.	Names of Contestants	BIRTH RECORD			Date of Enrollment for Present term	Year in School	No. periods recitation work successfully carried last semester	No. of periods recitation work successfully carried to date this semester	No. of years Student has competed in H.S. Athletics
		Mo. and Day	Year	County and State					
	Eihl, Young	4/6	1896	Rock Island, Ill.	9/8/14	4	20		
	Ackley, Robert	12/29	1896	Rock Island, Ill.	9/8/14	4	20	20	2
	Anderson, Robert	12/5	1896	Wright, Mo.	9/14/14	3	20	15	—
	Butler, Solomon	3/3	1895	King Fisher, Okla.	9/9/14	4	20	20	3
	Criswell, Raymond	10/19	1894	Rock Island, Ill.	9/14/14	5	20	20	2
	Dorring, Leo	5/7	1898	Madison, Ill.	9/8/14	4	21	19½	—
	Fennick, Edward	11/9	1897	Rock Island, Ill.	9/8/14	3	16	19½	1
	Hendren, Verne	4/20	1897	Rock Island, Ill.	9/8/14	4	16	21	—
	Hinckley, Arthur	4/29	1894	Rock Island, Ill.	9/8/14	4	16	25	2
	James, Edgar	9/29	1896	Livingston, Mo.	9/8/14	3	20	20	1
	Johnson, Leslie	3/12	1897	Rock Island, Ill.	9/8/14	4	20	20	1
	Klar, LeRoy	4/20	1896	LaSalle, Ill.	9/8/14	4	15	25	—
	Nichols, Joel	2/25	1896	Peoria, Ill.	9/8/14	3	22½	22½	—
	Punch, Bliss	8/21	1897	Rock Island, Ill.	9/8/14	4	21	21	2
	Reere, Fay	11/10	1895	Rock Island, Ill.	9/8/14	4	16	20	3
	Thomas, Ibrian	2/1	1897	Jackson, Iowa	9/8/14	3	21	24	2
	Whisler, Clifford	8/10	1895	Albany, Ill.	9/5/14	2	16	20	1
	Wagner, Leo	2/16	1896	Muscatine, Iowa	9/8/14	4	20	20	—
	Gartser, Ardo	12/2	1896	Rock Island, Ill.	9/8/14	3	18	20	1
	Looby, Frank	8/3	1896	Rock Island, Ill.	9/	4	16		1
	Gleason, Will	7/26	1896	Cook, Ill.	9/2		15	25	1
	Lindley, Keith	3/18	1895	McClean, Ill.	9/				
	Marks, Myer	4/4	1896	Rock Island, Ill.	9/8/14	3	15	20	—
	Culley, Will	1/22	1897	York, Ill.	9/8/14	3	20	20	

Eligibility roster for the 1914-15 season at Rock Island High School   Source- David Sebben

OLD RIVALS ARE READY FOR BIG GAME SATURDAY

DAVENPORT AND ROCK ISLAND CLASH FOR FIRST TIME IN SEVEN YEARS

WILL WATCH "SOL" BUTLER

Coach Nixon Trains His Battlers to Keep Their Eyes on the Islanders' Star—No Predictions Being Made

BEAT DAVENPORT IS POPULAR CRY IN ROCK ISLAND

Old Time Rival High School Elevens to Meet in First Game Since 1906.

ENTHUSIASM RUNS HIGH

Will Be Called Promptly at 2:30 at Three-Eye Park Across River— Direct Car Service Promised.

Coach Roe Says Islanders Win

The team is in first class condition and should play a hard, fast game. The line is doing good work and the backfield is faster than at anytime this year. There are few experienced men on the team, but all are working together. We have good substitutes and any man who doesn't do all he can will go to the sidelines. If Davenport doesn't play a much better game than they did last Saturday we will win by two touchdowns.

Coach H. N. Roe,
Rock Island Team.

With the weather conditions as favorable this Saturday as they were last, we will beat Davenport by two touchdowns. There is not a man on the team that is not in the best of condition. There is not a man on the Davenport team that we fear.

Captain A. Hinkley,
Rock Island Team.

Three I Field in Davenport where Butler played football against Davenport High. Source- Retro Quad Cities

On the day of the game, the Rock Island team arrived by streetcar at the Three I stadium on West 4th Street and Telegraph Road in Davenport. Shortly after play began at 2:35 p.m., it was evident that Coach Roe's boys were not going to measure up to the much larger team from Davenport High, since Rock Island was handicapped by about 13 pounds per player. The Islanders fought gallantly against the much bigger line and backs, but to no avail. When Rock Island was on offense, the ball was handed off to Butler over and over, but his advances were for short gains, because blocking for him was snubbed by the larger Davenport team.

Rock Island's football team traveled to Davenport by street car across the Government Bridge.

HARD TO STOP SOL

Former Hutchinson Colored Athlete Star at Rock Island, Ill.

PLAYS QUARTERBACK NOW

Coach Roe's Team Has Chance For Illinois High School Football Championship.

RED AND BLUE DEFEATS ISLANDERS SATURDAY, 21 TO 7

Rock Island Has Phenomenal Performer in "Sol" Butler—Puts up "One Man" Battle

Mr. Sol Butler is a world beater at playing football, so says the R. I. H. school boys and girls.

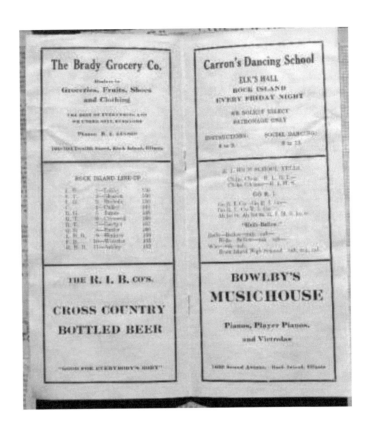

Actual football program from Davenport vs Rock Island game. Source- David Sebben

SOL. BUTLER MAKES SENSATION-AL PLAY FOR ROCK ISLAND

Big Crowd Out for Football Game on Davenport Field—Colored Boy Is Hero

The premier play of the day occurred during the first quarter. Butler was credited for a 95-yard touchdown run, although it was clear he stood in the end zone when he caught the ball, circled the goal posts, and advanced it for the score. This play genuinely excited the 3,000 fans attending the game. When Butler touched the ball, the Rock Island fans were on their feet, and the Davenport fans held their collective breath.

> A *Davenport Daily Times* reporter's account of Butler's touchdown...*The Davenport team to a man played good ball and succeeded in stopping most of their opponents' rushes. King went over for a touchdown after a series of linebucks from the center of the field. This was soon followed by the beautiful run by Butler. The big colored lad taking the ball behind his goal, ran the length of the field at a wonderful speed. Tomson headed him off and so did Shuler, but both were brushed aside.*

After this run, the Davenport defense was more cautious in handling Butler; and were lying in wait every time he touched the ball. Although Rock Island was defeated, 21-7, both schools were jubilant that this rivalry had been renewed.

The Islanders would present a completely different lineup when they faced the Maroons of Moline on November 14 at Browning Field. Blocking and running interference was practiced in the gymnasium, as was improved signal calling. Coach Roe seemed extremely pleased with the results. When Rock Island arrived at Moline, they were greeted by a huge crowd and goal posts decorated with maroon and white and crimson and gold streamers. Former Moline graduates raised enough money to hire a band to play, while Rock Island brought the school band along for support. This was also the first time these two teams had met in two years, since the rivalry had been cancelled due to trouble after a game in Moline back in 1912.

Moline Outweighs Islanders

ROCK ISLAND HIGH SCHOOL				MOLINE HIGH SCHOOL			
Position	Age	Wght.	Experience in Years	Position	Age	Wght.	Experience in Years
Looby, le	18	142	2	Willis,, re	20	149	3
Gleason, lt	18	163	2	Simonsen, rt	18	161	3
Nichols, lg	18	147	1	Lundberg, rg	18	164	3
Culley, c	17	144	1	Wilson, c	17	164	2
James, rg	18	151	1	Buelow, lg	18	145	2
Criswell, rt	20	151	3	Mullinix, lt	18	161	2
Gaetjer, re	17	160	2	Weiderquist, le	18	160	1
Johnson, qb	17	130	1	Harrah, qb	18	137	3
Butler, lhb	19	162	3	Peterson, rhb	19	153	2
Ackley, rhb	17	141	3	Ludwick, lhb	16	145	2
Whisler, fb	19	162	2	Woodyatt, fb	17	155	1
Average	18	149	1.90	Average	18	153	2.15
Backfield av'rage		146		Backfield av'rage		147½	
Average of line		151		Average of line		156 2-7	

By the recent change in lineup the red and gold team was made two pounds lighter to the man, Johnson, the new quarterback, being the lightest player on both teams. The weights given above are stripped weights.

Source- *Rock Island Argus*

"A special streetcar will leave Market Square in downtown Rock Island direct for the field at 1:30 p.m., with a second leaving at 1:45. More will be provided as needed. A large double trucked streetcar will leave the high school at 1:45, which will transport the band and the team. After the game, many cars will be available for the return trip to Rock Island." **-Source-** *Rock Island Argus*

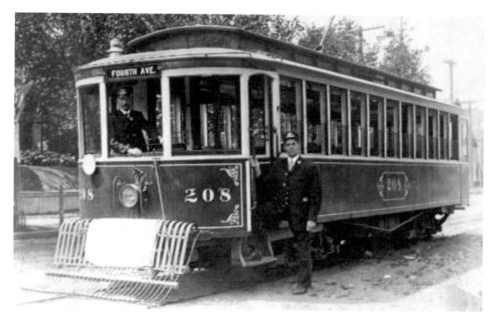

Street cars were the primary mode of transportation for high school football teams in Rock Island, Davenport, and Moline. Source- Retro Quad Cities

Coach Roe commented a day before the big game that *"regardless of how the 'dope' may stand, the interest in the Rock Island-Moline football game, to be played at Moline tomorrow, is probably greater than in any Tri-City contest in recent years. The teams, meeting for the first time in three seasons, are prepared for the supreme test, realizing that in a certain degree, the high school athletic supremacy of the two towns is at stake. Both teams are full of confidence and whatever the outcome may be, a wonderful game may be expected. Both teams use open formations and it is probable that long runs and trick plays will bring the fans to a state of frenzy."*

INTENSE INTEREST IN ROCK IS-LAND-MOLINE GAME SATURDAY

BUTLER PLAYING AT END POSITION

ROOTERS SURPRISED TO SEE ROCK ISLAND PERFORMER THERE

Game time was set at 2:30 p.m. at Browning Field before a large crowd of 5,000 excited fans. Teamwork was responsible for Rock Island's 12-0 victory over Moline. Every member of the team played as if it was the game of his life. The newly appointed quarterback, Leslie Johnson, proved his worth after being brought up from the second string.

With Coach Roe changing up his team's tactics, even the Rock Island fans were kept guessing as to what was going to happen. Everyone was surprised to see Butler starting at end, and eventually played every position in the backfield. Johnson, the new quarterback, followed Roe's instructions to the letter, and played like a veteran, picking apart the Moline defense with precision.

Gleason scored the first touchdown with Butler scoring the second. Butler played a magnificent game, plowing through the Plow Boys when running the ball, blocking, and in making some of the prettiest tackles ever witnessed at Browning Field. Moline fans were heard yelling, "Get Butler! Get Butler!"

Actual game ball used by Butler to score his touchdown against Moline, his last high school game

ROCK ISLAND IS WINNER 12 TO 0 IN BATTLE HERE

Rock Island, Doped to Lose, Wins by Playing the Better Ball.

Touchdowns Scored by Gleason and Butler in Second Half and Moline Is Defeated.

MOLINE IS OUT OF THE RUNNING

ROCK ISLAND KILLS ITS CHANCES FOR STATE CHAMPIONSHIP

Browning Field in Moline as it would have appeared when Butler played

Although the weather had been extremely dry in the fall, the field was a muddy bog that severely restricted long runs around the ends. Both teams slipped and stumbled during the game. Moline school officials stated that the field had been "sprinkled to settle the dust," but was later learned that they had intentionally muddied the field, with the assistance of the Moline Fire Department, in an attempt to slow down Butler. After the game, one of the referees, K.M. Patterson of Chicago, was interviewed and was amazed at the athleticism of Butler. *"The score was 0-0 and it was late in the third quarter and Butler had just completed a long end run that put the ball at Moline's three-yard line. He was given the ball again and it appeared he was going to kick the ball, but instead leaped at the linemen and Moline stood him up. No gain. The next play, he stood about two yards further back and at express speed, ran at the line and leaped about seven feet in the air, over both the offense and defensive lines. He did not hurdle, as he went over headfirst and landed three feet beyond the goal line. You should have seen the look of astonishment on the faces of the Moline lads. I had never seen such a play in all my years of officiating; and would probably never will again if I do this for the next 50 years."*

BUTLER MAKES GREATEST PLAY

TOUCHDOWN IN MOLINE WON-DERFUL SAYS NOTED REFEREE

MOLINE OUTPLAYED

COLD FIGURES SHOW THAT IS LANDERS HAD EDGE IN EVERY WAY.

Victors Gained Total of 543 Yards and Moline Only 290—Hangs Some Profit Realized.

This was Butler's last high school football game, Rock Island finished 6-2 for the season, scoring 254 points and giving up only 49 points, and claiming a mythical state championship. The final game of the season, to be played against Aurora High School, was cancelled due to multiple injuries on the team, and parental intervention about football being a violent sport. Ackley was hospitalized after getting kicked in the kidney, while several others were nursing significant injuries. After the Moline game, Butler reflected on a favorite poem he had written:

"Whichever way the wind doth blow, some heart is glad to have it so. Then blow it east or blow it west, the wind that blows-that wind is best."

These words would prove to be very prophetic in Butler's life.

That evening after the game, a large bonfire was torched on the Rock Island riverfront in celebration of the victory over Moline. The Rock Island High School band paraded down 2nd Avenue and performed at the bonfire. Coach Roe and many of the players gave a recap of the game and festivities to the crowd of over 2,000 well-wishers. Many Moline fans and players attended as well.

The Moline High School senior class was so impressed with Butler's prowess on the field, that they composed a song about him that was performed on their senior class day in May. These are the lyrics, as provided by the Moline High School library:

His name was Solomon Butler

In Kansas he won fame;

So they brought him to Illinois

To play Rock Island's game.

He played a brand of football,

The finest ever seen,

But play the best that Solomon could

He couldn't beat Moline.

Chorus—Oh, Solomon Butler

What are you going to do?

Poor Solomon Butler

When we get after you.

He played a brand of football,

The finest ever seen.

But play the best that Solomon could,

He couldn't beat Moline.

The lyrics weren't quite accurate since Rock Island had beaten Moline in 1914. Below is another song composed by Moline students about Butler— (sung to the tune of Farewell Ladies)

So long Butler, so long Butler, so long Butler,

We're going to leave you now.

We hate to leave you very bad, very bad, very bad;

We hate to leave you very bad,

Since you're just a one-man team.

Farewell Butler, farewell Butler, farewell Butler,

You'll eat our dust today.

We think a whole lot of your speed, of your speed, of your speed;

We think a whole lot of your speed,

But think more of our team.

Good night Butler, good night Butler, good night Butler,

Eleven to one's not fair.

But since Rock Island can't scare up a team, scare up a team, scare up a team;

Since Rock Island can't scare up a team,

We'll have to beat the best they have.

Butler would earn a high spot as fullback on the Illinois All-State football team and was lauded as the greatest prep player ever in the state of Illinois.

Critics Pick "Sol" Butler for Halfback—Fastest High School Man
In the Country

Is Given a Place on
the All-State Team

Sol Butler,
Rock Island high school player is touted as greatest prep player in Illinois.

Butler's transition from Hutchinson, Kansas to Rock Island, Illinois had been a smooth one, with all existing permissions at that time being legal and forthright. However, several schools complained that Rock Island High School had an unfair advantage with Butler on its team. In November of 1914, an Illinois High School Association by-law was written up that would have prohibited such a move.

WOULD HAVE KEPT BUTLER OUT

Butler would have been eliminated from the Rock Island high school athletics if the new by-law, which the State Athletic association made at a recent meeting, was put in effect this fall. The law reads: "No person whose parents are not residents of the school district in which he is attending school shall be permitted to represent that school until he shall have been in attendance one year, excepting students coming from districts having no accredited high schools, which offer one year, two years or three years of work." According to this law, Butler would have been ruled out of athletics here, as he came here in the fall, as his parents reside in Hutchinson, Kans. The new by-law will take effect next fall.

November 23, 1914   *Davenport Daily Times*

CLINCH CHAMPIONSHIP.

Coach Herbert Roe's Rock Island Team Won Yesterday.

A telegram was received here last night by a friend of Coach Herbert Roe of the Rock Island, Ill., high school football team. It told of Rock Island's 12 to 0 victory over Moline, which virtually clinches the state championship. No mention was made by Roe of the work of Sol Butler, the fleet negro youth who played with Hutchinson two years.

The Hutchinson Gazette continued to follow Butler's career while at Rock Island.

After football season, Butler sang second tenor with the Rock Island High School Men's Glee Club. It was reported that he had a magnificent singing voice, and his brother Benjamin's was even better.

Rock Island High School Men's Glee Club-Solomon is in back row on the right   Source- *Watch Tower* **yearbook**

In December, he would receive an invitation to participate in the Pan-American Games to be held in San Francisco on August 6-7, 1915.

Sol and his brother Ben returned to Hutchinson for Christmas break and while there, Butler was asked how football compared in Illinois versus Kansas. "We won the state championship this year and the football elevens in the east are heavier and play harder than those in this country. The team work is better and the coaches train the players to follow a certain system. The game follows the college style closer all the way through," he said with his usual smile. The brothers returned to Rock Island on January 8 to continue with their studies. Due to its proximity to where Butler lived, he spent many hours at the Rock Island Public Library studying his favorite subject….history.

Interior views of Rock Island High School where Butler attended his senior year.   Source- Rock Island County Historical Society

ASSEMBLY ROOM – ROCK ISLAND HIGH SCHOOL.

LIBRARY – ROCK ISLAND HIGH SCHOOL.

When not competing in sports, Butler spent many hours in these two rooms, singing and studying.

MOB TEAM AT MT. CARROLL

Rock Islanders Require Guard to Escort Them to Hotel

Reports reached Rock Island today telling of a narrow escape from being mobbed, experienced by the Rock Island high school basket ball team at Mt. Carroll last night. Rock Island won the game, 28 to 27. Butler, the colored athlete, played a star part. Something peeved the Mt. Carroll crowd and they hooted the Rock Island players and made things so unpleasant that the Islanders stayed in the gymnasium until 11 o'clock before going to the hotel. A number of the Mt. Carroll boys acted as an escort on the trip to the hotel.

Rock Island 80; alumni 32.
Rock Island 19; Sterling 21.
Rock Island 48; faculty 22.
Rock Island 38; Tiskilwa 12.
Rock Island 19; Moline 17.
Rock Island 46; Geneseo 28.
Rock Island 43; Cambridge 11.
Rock Island 24; Davenport 31.
Rock Island 28; Mt. Carroll 27.
Rock Island 19; Davenport 21.
Rock Island 85; Aledo 27.
Rock Island 52; Moline 17.
Score in the district tournament at Galesburg:
Rock Island 30; Knoxville 10.
Rock Island 43; Farmington 25.
Rock Island 25; Aledo 20.
Rock Island 2; Princeville 2. (Forfeit.)
Rock Island 29; Galesburg 10.
In the state tournament:
Rock Island 19; Springfield 21.
Total number of points—Rock Island 517; opponents 347.

ISLANDER FIVE OUT FOR TITLE

WIN RIGHT TO COMPETE IN THE STATE TOURNEY THIS MONTH

Win Four Straight Games in Semi-Finals at Galesburg—Butler and Reeves Are Individual Stars

Rock Island's 1914-15 basketball schedule

1914-15 Rock Island basketball team   Source- *Watch Tower* yearbook

The Islanders would go 15-4 for the season and Butler would score a total of 55 points. Although he didn't score a lot of points during the season, his quick step on defense was his strong suite, and opposing teams hated playing against him. On January 19, Coach Roe staged a basketball game at the high school between the seniors and the freshman. While the seniors thought it would be an easy game, they had their subs play first. However, the freshman put up a good battle, and Roe finally placed the starting seniors on the court, with Butler leading the way. Yet, the freshman outscored the upperclassmen and won 29-23. A reporter for the Davenport *Daily Times* noted that during the January 22 game at Moline, Butler was clearly outjumped by Weiderquist of Moline and was perhaps, the poorest basket tosser on the floor. Butler would miss the second Moline game due to being at a track meet in Chicago, and because he was ruled ineligible due to back studies, he did not play against Geneseo. On March 2, the Avon High School basketball coach filed a complaint against Rock Island, saying that Butler and Gleason's names did not appear on the official roster. Just days prior, Avon was disqualified from the Galesburg tournament after beating Abingdon, but it was proven that an Avon player's name did not appear on the official roster of that game. Rock Island proved the dispute to be false.

March 9, 1915, was an extremely gloomy day at Rock Island, but not due to the weather. Local sports enthusiasts were in shock. Butler had turned his basketball uniform in to Coach Robb the night before and stated he would not be making the trip to Decatur to play in the state tournament game.

Rock Island faced Springfield High School in Decatur on March 11, 1915 and ended up losing in overtime 21-19, with the Governor's son hitting the winning basket. Hopes for a state championship were lost. Had Butler played in Decatur, the hotel where Rock Island was staying at made it clear that he could not stay there with the team, due to his skin color. After the state tournament, in which he did not play, Butler stated to the media that the reason he did not participate wasn't because of lack of loyalty or spirit for the Crimson and Gold, but because of an examination he had prior to the Davenport game. A physician that examined his knee said it was in very bad condition and advised Solomon to quit basketball if he truly wanted to focus on track in the spring. Yet, despite the injury and warning from the doctor and Coach Roe, Butler played in the Davenport game, which further aggravated the knee. A second exam prior to the state tournament proved that Sol was in no condition to play. Friends and fans understood the decision, since Butler was using his athletic abilities to secure a college education, and further injury may have prevented this. Butler gave everything due to his loyalty to Rock Island High School and Coaches Robb and Roe.

In February of 1915, Butler, along with his brother Ben, wrote and published a 53-page book about his track and football experiences and training methods named *Three Years in High School Athletics*. The book was published by the Driffill Printing Company of Rock Island, IL. Butler's father received a shipment of the books and sold them in Hutchinson. "Sol's book is going to be here on March 15, and I'm going to sell them to white folks and black folks too", his father mused. When asked what was in the book, he said, "I ain't seen the book yet, but I know it is good. Just think of the source." Butler had hoped that the proceeds from the book would be sufficient to attend Harvard, but sales did not live up to his expectations. Only several hundred copies were sold. (*Today, there is only one known copy of his book.*)

The first track meet of the 1915 season was the 21st Annual Eighth Regiment Armory Indoor Meet in Chicago, with Butler being the sole representative from Rock Island High School. Sol finished fourth overall and received the individual cup among 431 athletes. At this meet, he beat Joe Loomis for first place in the 40-yard dash, first in the 300-yard dash, and the 40-yard hurdles.

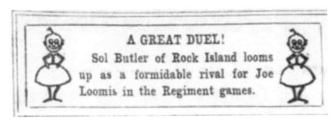

The Eighth Regiment Armory was brand new when Sol competed here

At the Northwestern Indoor Meet on March 26-27, 1915, the Rock Island track team of Solomon Butler, Vivian Thomas, Frank Miller, and Ulysses Clark participated against several hundred athletes from throughout the Midwest. Butler finished first in the 60-yard dash in 6.25 seconds (tying the world record): 5 yards ahead of the second place finisher; first in the 60-yard high hurdles in 8 seconds (setting a world record); first in the broad jump with a leap of 21 feet, 11 inches; and first in the shot put with a heave of 45 feet. He chose not to participate in the high jump, but when challenged by other athletes, he jumped the bar at 5 feet, 10 inches-- in his street clothes. By the conclusion of the meet, Butler had 20 individual points, winning the individual cup and bringing home a first-place team trophy for Rock Island.

BUTLER EQUALS WORLD RECORD FOR 60 YARDS

Feat of Rock Island Negro Features Games Held at Northwestern.

NEGRO BOY TIES RECORD

Runs Sixty Yards in Six and Two-fifths Seconds.

Chicago, March 27. Sol. Butler, of Rock Island, Ill., a negro, equalled the world's record for the sixty-yard dash last night in the preliminary try-outs of the sixth annual indoor interscholastic meet at Northwestern University. Butler ran the distance in 6 2-5 seconds.

ISLANDERS TO RESCUE

TRACK TEAM IN SHAPE OF SOL BUTLER TO REHABILITATE PURPLE ATHLETICS.

Star Negro Sprinter, Who Captured Northwestern Meet, to Enter that School Next Fall.

Beginning this fall Northwestern university expects to gain a higher place in athletic events of all kinds under control of the intercollegiate conference and regain in some branches of sport the renown it had two decades ago when Potter and Van Doozer brought victory to the Methodist university on many a football field.

This expectation was given a start yesterday when it was announced by Athletic Director Omer that the Rock Island track and field team would enter Northwestern next fall. This track team, in the person of Sol Butler, won the interscholastic indoor meet at Patten gymnasium in Evanston Saturday night.

Butler was accompanied to Chicago by several other pupils from the Rock Island school, but none of them was able to score any points. Butler won the meet unaided. He took four first places, scoring twenty points, which gave his school first place.

In these events he equaled the world's indoor record for the sixty yard high hurdles and surpassed other records which he himself had made at Patten gymnasium when he was with the Hutchinson (Kas.) high school team.

Star in Other Sports.

Butler will be graduated from Rock Island next June. In September he will enter Northwestern university. Under the conference rules he will not be eligible to represent the school in athletics until his sophomore year.

In his high school career Butler also has been as proficient in football, baseball, and basketball.

This article appeared in the Moline *Daily Dispatch* on March 31, 1915

Prior to this meet, Lewis Institute filed a claim on March 24 with Northwestern University that Solomon was 21 years old and not 20 as he claimed. Race director Omer started an investigation to discover the truth in this matter by contacting officials in Kingfisher, Oklahoma and Hutchinson, Kansas. Records from Butler's former homes proved his correct age.

Sol Butler to Enter Northwestern in Fall

Hutchinson Negro Athlete Will Graduate from Rock Island High School This Spring.

This headline in the April 7, 1915 *Hutchinson Gazette* eventually proved to be wrong.

On April 24, the annual Rock Island High School inter-class track meet was held at Exposition Park. The seniors came out on top with a score of 57, the juniors with 45, the sophomores with 20, and the freshmen with nine points.

On a bad track and against a stiff wind, Ben Butler won the 50-yard dash and Sol took first in the 100-yard dash with a time of 10.2 seconds, and first in the 220-yard dash with a time of 22.2 seconds.

The remains of the indoor track at the Rock Island YMCA where Butler trained during the winter months of 1914-15.
Source- David Sebben

Knox College hosted the 7th annual Big 8 Interscholastic Track and Field Meet on May 1, 1915 in Galesburg, Illinois. Here, on the campus where Abraham Lincoln and Stephen Douglas once debated, Butler placed first in the 50 yard dash with a time of 5.25 seconds, equaling the world record; first in the 100 yard dash at 10 seconds; first in the broad jump with a leap of 20 feet, 10 ¾ inches; second in the 220 yard low hurdles at 26 seconds; and second in the shot put. Record crowds that attended the meet followed Butler from event to event; interested in what he was going to do next. Davenport placed first in team points with 33, while Rock Island finished second with 30 points. With 23 points, Butler won the individual cup.

The actual program from the Big 8 Interscholastic track and field meet at Knox College in 1915. David Sebben collection

While living in Rock Island, Butler and his brother Ben attended the Second Baptist Church.

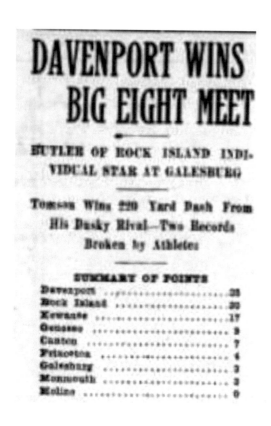

DAVENPORT WINS BIG EIGHT MEET

BUTLER OF ROCK ISLAND INDIVIDUAL STAR AT GALESBURG

Tomson Wins 220 Yard Dash From His Dusky Rival—Two Records Broken by Athletes

SUMMARY OF POINTS

Davenport 28
Rock Island 26
Kewanee 17
Geneseo 9
Canton 7
Princeton 6
Galesburg 3
Monmouth 3
Moline 0

MOLINE HAS NO CHANCE TO WIN TRI-CITY MEET

Competition Next Saturday to Be Between Davenport and Rock Island.

BUTLER WILL PERFORM

His Only Appearance in Tri-Cities — Staged at Exposition Park.

Rock Island hosted the 8th annual Tri-City Track and Field Meet at Exposition Park on May 8, 1915, with Davenport and Moline participating. Butler won the 50-yard dash, the 100-yard dash, high hurdles, the broad jump (setting a record at 21 feet, 5 ¼ inches). He finished second in the shot put and discus. Davenport won the event with 68 points, Rock Island placed second with 55, and Moline placed third with 11 points. Butler won individual honors with 31 points. This was the one and only time Butler competed in a track meet in Rock Island and a record crowd turned out to witness history.

As a student at Rock Island High School, Butler spent a lot of time studying at the Rock Island Public Library.

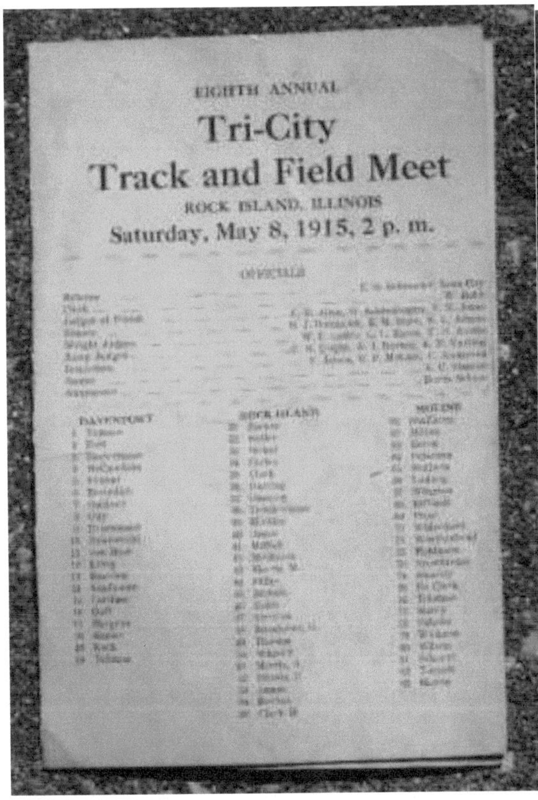

EIGHTH ANNUAL

Tri-City
Track and Field Meet
ROCK ISLAND, ILLINOIS
Saturday, May 8, 1915, 2 p. m.

OFFICIALS

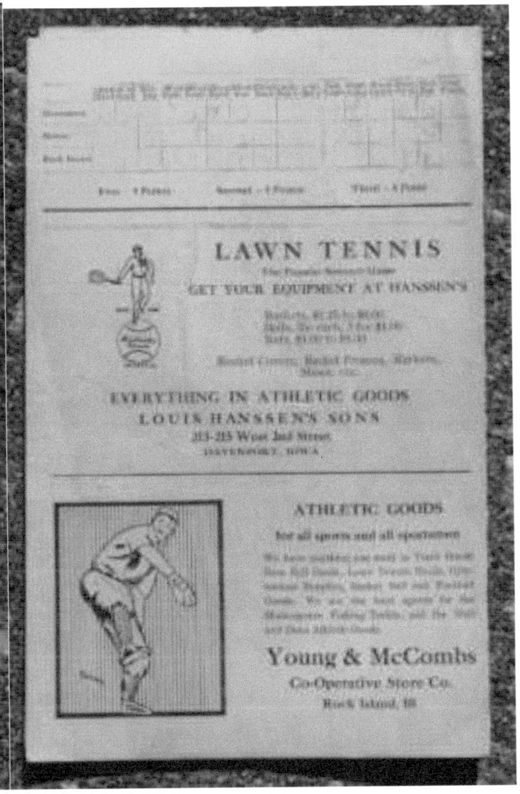

LAWN TENNIS
GET YOUR EQUIPMENT AT HANSSEN'S

EVERYTHING IN ATHLETIC GOODS
LOUIS HANSSEN'S SONS
213-215 West 2nd Street
DAVENPORT, IOWA

ATHLETIC GOODS
for all sports and all spectators

Young & McCombs
Co-Operative Store Co.
Rock Island, Ill.

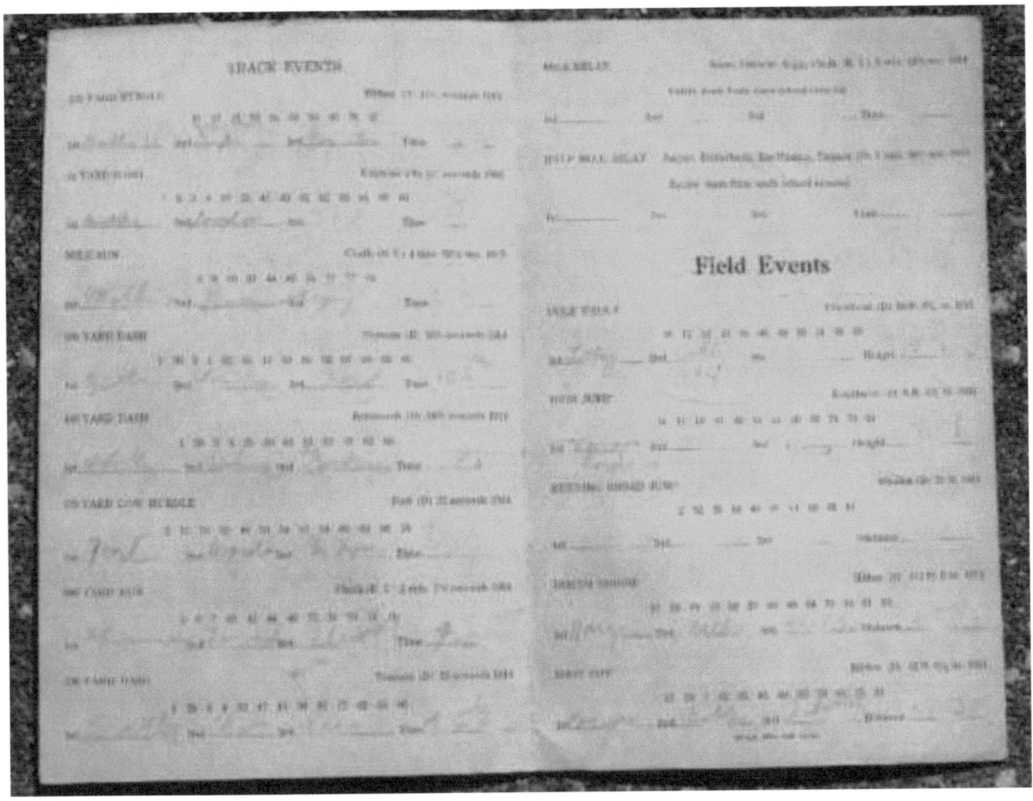

TRACK EVENTS

Field Events

Actual 1915 Tri-City Track and Field Meet program   Source- David Sebben collection

Rock Island Exposition Park, home to Rock Island High School track and football

The Exposition Park grandstands, on the southwest corner of 9th Street and 18th Avenue. Not only was it home to Rock Island High School football and track, it was the county fairgrounds. Source-Retro Quad Cities

Coach Herbert Roe, Sol Butler, and Ben Butler show off the awards Sol earning during his high school career. Sol was very proud of his accomplishments, but was never boastful. Source - *Watch Tower* yearbook

1915 Rock Island High School Track Team   Source- *Watch Tower* **yearbook**

Butler and the Islanders traveled west on May 15, 1915 to Iowa City, Iowa to be at the 8th annual Iowa University Interscholastic Track Meet. For unknown reasons, Rock Island chose not to participate in the Illinois Interscholastic Meet in Urbana, Illinois on this date; although earlier in the month, newspaper accounts reported that Rock Island would attend. But it was later learned that, due to the proximity of Iowa City to Rock Island, and that the Iowa meet personally invited Butler to showcase him and the Rock Island track team, Rock Island would be the only non-Iowa school to compete here.

Even though heavy rains marred the event, Butler won the 100-yard dash, the 220-yard dash, and the 220-yard low hurdles, and set a meet record in the broad jump with a leap of 22 feet, 2 ½ inches. The old record was 21 feet, ¾ inches. He finished second in the shot put and in the half mile relay, running the last lap in 22 seconds. Davenport finished with 28 1/3 points, with Rock Island and West Des Moines tying for second place with 27 points. Butler collected 23 of the points by himself. A large number of Rock Island supporters made the trip by automobile and by bicycle, a trip of 62 miles each way.

Sol Butler, the colored schoolboy wonder of Rock Island High School, scored 23 points in the Iowa State interscholastic meet at Iowa City, Ia, Saturday. He won four firsts and one second. In the broad jump he cleared 22ft 2½in. The winning school scored only five more points than Butler.

Boston Globe

River to River Road (Highway 6)- Source- IDOT Historic Photo Collection

SOL BUTLER THE STAR IN IOWA TRACK MEET

He Broke a Jump Record and Did Some Neat Running.

SOL GETS 23 POINTS

BUTLER OF ROCK ISLAND WINS FIELD CHAMPIONSHIP IN IOWA CITY MEET.

Leaps 22 Feet 2½ Inches in the Running Broad Jump—" Is First.

The *Rock Island Argus* wrote this account of Butler's events in Iowa City, "*Sol Butler early became the center of attention, as he easily qualified in all of the events in which he was entered. The distance by which he led in the dashes caused much comment, while a trial jump of 22 feet 4 inches in the running broad jump electrified the crowd. Sol proved the only Rock Island man to qualify in the events of the morning.*

In the running broad jump, Sol broke the record with a jump of 22 feet 2 ½ inches. This leap bested the old record of 21 feet ¾ inch, set by Rhodes of Davenport in 1914, by a foot and ¼ inch. The interest of the crowd throughout was centered on Butler, who in each of his events gave an exhibition of racing never seen before by the track fans at the meet. Sol annexed three more points in the shotput by copping second place, but he failed to place in the discus. Coach Roe did not enter a team in the mile relay, but in the half mile relay Clark, Jones, Thomas and Butler was the squad selected to represent the local school. Butler's finish in this race was an exhibition of the most wonderful running ever witnessed on the university field. Clark, the first man for Rock Island, ran a close third, while Jones, in his 220, slipped back into fifth position. Thomas, the third man, also lost winding up in seventh position about 35 yards from the leading man. Sol then took up the race set the crowd wild by passing up the five men in front of him in short order. He then gave all that was in him in an endeavor to pass the Cedar Rapids man who was leading, and he cut down yard after yard of his opponent's lead. But the average was just a little too great and the race a little too short for Sol to overcome the 35 yard lead, and the Cedar Rapids man breasted the tape about a foot in advance of the colored streak. Experienced track officials said after the meet that they never had seen and never expected to see again such an exhibition of running as Sol exhibited. One of the timers stated that Sol made the 220 in 21 2-5 seconds, a wonderful record."

Iowa Field, site of the Iowa Interscholastic track meet   Source—University of Iowa Digital Library

"It is not wealth, or rank, or state, but 'get up and get' that makes men great."— Sol Butler

Butler received a letter from a former Rock Island High School student, now attending Grinnell College, and told him that a group of track enthusiasts offered to subsidize his expenses for participating at a track meet on May 29, 1915, but due to heavy rains the day before, he opted to skip the event and would rest up for the Stagg meet on June 12.

At the beginning of the football season in 1914, the high school's athletic association had a mere $30 in its account, but due to the popularity of Butler in football, basketball and track, they ended the school year with over $1000 in its coffers.

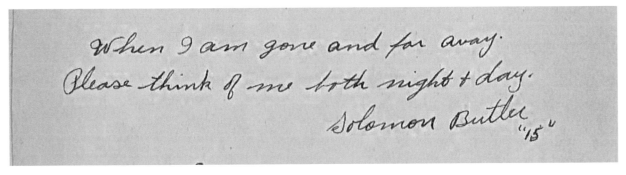

Solomon Butler's actual signature from a 1915 Rock Island High School scrapbook. Source-David Sebben collection

Northwestern University will get Sol Butler, the colored boy, who is the athletic marvel of the middle west. He may eclipse Howard Drew.

April 12, 1915   *Miami Herald*

BUTLER MAKES GREAT RECORD

SCORES 112 POINTS FOR ROCK IS-LAND IN FIVE MEETS

Copped Individual Honors at All Meets
—Plans Being Formed to Send
Him to the Exposition

DAVENPORT WINS IN TRACK MEET

ROCK ISLAND AND DES MOINES TIED FOR SECOND PLACE

Butler Makes 23 of the 24 Points for
His School—Hargens
Is Star

BUTLER SHINES IN LAST MEET

Closes Track Work for Rock Island by Great Exhibition

Sol Butler, colored track star of Rock Island, in the last meet in which he will compete as a representative of the local school, won second place for Rock Island at Iowa City Saturday He won 23 of Rock Island's 24 points. Butler has made 77 points in the last three meets, 23 at Galesburg, 31 in the tri-city meet, and 23 at Iowa City. He is the best all around athlete the Rock Island school has ever had. A complete account of the Iowa City meet appears on another page of The Times today.

TRACK MEET TO DAVENPORT; BUTLER STAR OF CONTESTS.

Iowa City, Ia., May 15—(Special.)—Decided in the final event, the eighth annual state interscholastic meet, the closest in the history of the classic, was won this afternoon on Iowa field by Davenport High with 28 1-3 points as against 27 each by West Des Moines and Rock Island.

Butler, the Rock Island negro athlete, scored 23 points. He won four firsts and one second, capturing the field championship. He smashed one state record, raising the running broad jump from 21 ft. ¾ in. to 22 ft. 2½ in.

FINALS SHOW SPEED THOUGH TRACK IS BAD

Interscholastic Field Meet Proves Successful Despite Inclement Weather.

COLORED MEN ARE FAST

Butler Captures Honors and H. Lovelle is Right Behind Him—Track Slow.

PRELIMINARIES IN FIELD MEET ON IOWA COURSE

Eliminating Process Trims Down List of Contestants in Iowa State Battle.

COLORED MAN IS A STAR

Butler, Rock Island Prodigy, Shows Form as Expected in His Various Events.

This wonderful photo of Sol was taken by student photographer Albert Crampton from Moline High School. The 15-year old Albert walked up to Sol at the Big Eight Interscholastic Track and Field Meet on May 3, 1915 on the campus of Knox College in Galesburg, Illinois, and asked if he could take his picture. Albert also saw Sol play his last high school football game when Rock Island defeated Moline 12-0. This photo is courtesy of Albert's grandson, Peter Rosene, an attorney in Minneapolis who graciously donated this photo to the author.

In an article in May 21, 1915 issue of the Davenport *Daily Times*, it was noted that *"Solomon Butler had scored 112 points in five meets this season, and in each meet, copped individual honors. At the Northwestern meet, he single-handedly won the meet with 20 points. This feat has never been equaled by any athlete in the world and much credit is due him. In his four years of high school, he has never entered a track meet where he did not capture individual honors."*

R. I. WILL LOSE SERVICES OF ROE

EFFICIENT HIGH SCHOOL COACH TO HAND IN RESIGNATION

Announcement Regretted By All Students—Will Accept Position In University

Coach Herbert N. Roe, of the Rock Island high school, has finally decided not to return to the local school next year. This announcement will bring regret to all the students as well as the faculty and alumni, as Coach Roe was considered one of the most efficient coaches Rock Island has ever had. He will present his resignation to the board of education soon. During the past year Rock Island was represented on the gridiron, basketball floor and track with the best teams that ever fought for the crimson and gold.

Receives Good Offers

Roe has not decided where he will coach next season but he has received good offers from several universities. As soon as school closes here in June he will accept a position as physical director at the South Park Play Grounds and Park System in Chicago. His former high school coach is at the head of the system. Sol Butler, whom coach Roe has developed into the best athlete in the United States, will also be given employment in Chicago. Roe will coach Butler again next year at which ever college the famous all around athlete will enter.

Athletics Run High

Mr. Roe spent most of his time training the high school teams and on the side developed football, basket ball and baseball teams among the younger students. The Rock Island high school never before witnessed such high class athletics as was played this year. The football team was far above its usual standard, as was the basket ball team. The track team was the best Rock Island has ever had. All the teams were developed through the hard work of Roe.

At the opening of the football team the treasury had only $30 and at the end over $1,000 was realized. Much interest was taken by all the Rock Island people in the school athletes because of the excellent teams developed.

This year's letter men of the Rock Island high school track team met in the athletic board of control's room last evening and Vivian Thomas was unanimously elected track captain for the coming season. Without a doubt Thomas has one of the hardest problems to face and overcome before he is able to gather together a winning track team next season than any track captain so far, for the track material in the high school which will remain for the next season was never at such a low ebb. Of the five letter men on the team this year Thomas and Jones are the only two who will be seen in track suits for the crimson and gold next season. Butler, Clark and Miller the other three, will graduate in June.

The loss of Coach Roe would be devasting for Rock Island High School. Not only did he bring worldwide fame to the track program, the football and basketball programs would both suffer. Rumors abounded that he had received offers from major universities and colleges, others stated he would follow Butler to coach him at Dubuque German College.

THE TRACK TEAM OF 1915

Roe would end up in Houston, Texas, coaching and teaching at Rice University in 1915. After one year at Rice, Roe then moved to the Army and later moved back to Hutchinson where he worked for a real estate company. Roe was quoted in 1919, "This is the first time in 15 years I have not played or coached football. I played all the time in high school and college and since then I have coached. While in the Army I decided there wasn't enough future to the coaching business and decided to change." Roe passed away in 1927.

Sol's yearbook from Rock Island High School   Source- David Sebben collection

Sol and Ben Butler's attendance ledger from their senior year.   Source - Rock Island High School Library Archives

The Class of Nineteen Hundred Fifteen

Rock Island High School

announces the

Exercises of Commencement Week

May thirtieth to June fifth

Rock Island Illinois

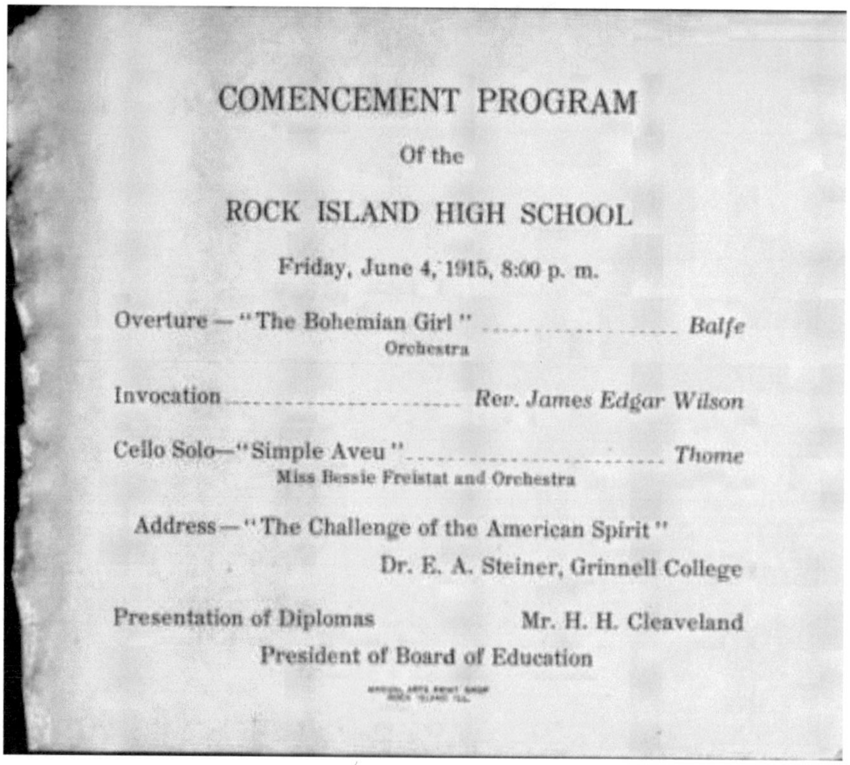

COMENCEMENT PROGRAM

Of the

ROCK ISLAND HIGH SCHOOL

Friday, June 4, 1915, 8:00 p. m.

Overture — "The Bohemian Girl" .... *Balfe*
Orchestra

Invocation .... *Rev. James Edgar Wilson*

Cello Solo—"Simple Aveu" .... *Thome*
Miss Bessie Freistat and Orchestra

Address — "The Challenge of the American Spirit"
Dr. E. A. Steiner, Grinnell College

Presentation of Diplomas   Mr. H. H. Cleaveland
President of Board of Education

Commencement announcements for Sol's graduation   Source- David Sebben collection

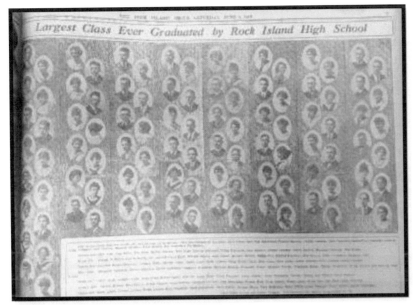

Solomon Butler graduated with the largest class to date (101) to earn their diplomas. The Empire Theater in downtown Rock Island hosted the ceremony on June 4 at 8 p.m. After graduation, Northwestern University's Coach Omer announced that Butler would attend NU in the fall, but this did not happen. Rumors spread that he would attend Harvard Law School.

After Butler graduated, he represented Rock Island High School at the University of Chicago Invitational Track and Field meet on June 12, a national meet that attracted 700 athletes from 132 schools in 18 states. Yet, prior to this meet, controversy over Butler's age reared its head again, with several Chicago area high schools considering a ban on the meet if Butler were to participate due to his alleged ineligible age. The issue went so far as going to the Department of the Interior, Bureau of Pensions Division, to see evidence of Butler's age.

TFD

OFFICE OF
THE COMMISSIONER

DEPARTMENT OF THE INTERIOR

BUREAU OF PENSIONS

WASHINGTON

June 10, 1915.

Mr. A. J. Burton,
   Rock Island,
      Illinois.

Sir:

In reply to your telegram of today, I have to advise you that it does not appear from an examination of the papers in the pension case, Certificate No.1046648, Benjamin Butler, alias Benjamin Bulison, Co. B, 2nd Iowa Infantry, that there is any evidence whatever on file as to the date of birth of Solomon Butler (or Butter) or Ben Butler, Jr.   As a matter of fact, the date of birth of the soldier himself is not clearly or distinctly shown.

Your telegram shows the name as <u>Butter</u>, but I presume Butler was the name intended.

It is not regarded as expedient to send you a reply by telegraph, as requested.

Very truly yours,

E. C. Tieman

Acting Commissioner.

Proof had to be given again and it was proven that Butler was of high school age to attend the meet.   Here is the actual letter from the Oak Park, Illinois High School principal, detailing his thoughts on the matter.

Oak Park, Ill.

June 8, 1912

Prin. A. J. Burton,

Rock Island. Ill.

My dear Burton:

There is considerable agitation among all the high schools around Chicago to get boys to refuse to compete in athletics against your man Butler on the ground that he is over age. I was told tonight that four or five leading schools are to tell Coach Stagg tomorrow that they will not compete in the University of Chicago interscholastic on Saturday if Butler is allowed to run.

When asked to join in this protest I refused because there is not sufficient evidence to support the charge.

Now if these schools make the protest in that final way I suspect that Stagg will forbid Butler to run. I hope that you are provided with the proper data to show that Butler is under the age limit. It is claimed that he was barred from all interscholastics in Kansas because of his age, even though the school records showed him to be under 21. These records are supposed to be those of his brother and it is claimed that he is using his brother's name at your school.

I am writing you merely that you may know the the general feeling around Chicago. Personally I think all such charges should be made direct to the principal of the school in question, as it is he who signs up for the eligibility of his boys.

I was surprised that you did not enter a team in the Illinois interscholastic as that would have corrected the impression that your school is represented by Butler only, and that you are not merely working for his advertisement.

Wishing you continued success in the educational work

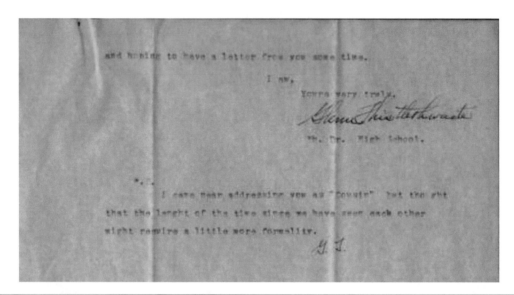

and hoping to have a letter from you some time.

I am,

Yours very truly,

Glenn Thistlethwaite

Mr. Dr. High School.

M.D.

I came near addressing you as "Cousin" but thought
that the length of the time since we have seen each other
might require a little more formality.

G.T.

PUBLIC HIGH SCHOOL.
A. J. BURTON, Principal
Rock Island, Illinois

Telegram.

Hutchinson Kas. 10 38 am June 10

A. J. Burton, Rock Island, Ill.
School records also school census records for several
years show birth date of Solomon Butler to be March Third
Eighteen Hundred Ninety Five.

J. O. Hall,
Supt. City Schools.

Butler was once again expected to dominate the meet in the 50-yard dash, 100-yard dash, low hurdles, broad jump, shot put, and discus. A local athlete, Lloyd Smart from LaGrange High School, was expected to be a contender, along with Brook Brewer from National Cathedral School in Washington, D.C., Collier from Marquette, Kansas; Bradford from Aledo, Illinois, and Crawford Carter, formerly of Rock Island High School, now attending National Cathedral.

Heavy rains prior to the event slowed down race times, and strong southerly winds during the event also hampered the elite runners. Butler was defeated in the 100-yard dash at the tape by E. Pearson of Spokane, Washington with a time of 10.15 seconds, but beat Pearson in the 220-yard dash with a time of 22.35 seconds. Butler finished second in the broad jump and finished with 13 overall points, tying Pearson for individual honors.

Stagg Field, University of Chicago   **Photo courtesy of University of Chicago**

E. Pearson, North Central High, Spokane; Solomon Butler, Rock Island High, R. Filter, East Division High, Milwaukee; R. Lock, Shaw High, East Cleveland, and G. Rausch, Waterloo.   Photo courtesy of University of Chicago

Solomon Butler, Rock Island High; E. Pearson, North Central High, Spokane; R. Filter, East Division High, Milwaukee; and Williamson, Watertown, S.D.   Photo courtesy of University of Chicago

ROCK ISLAND WILL NOT HAVE BUTLER IN 1915

Rock Island high school's assistance from Sol Butler in winning football games will be confined to the season now past. The colored star from Hutchinson, Kas., has played his last of high school football because of the fact that he will graduate next spring.

His ability as an athlete will be used to good account by the Islanders in the two other branches of high school sport, however, as he is a star in basketball and track. He won the sprints at Stagg's big meet in Chicago last June and is expected to repeat the coming spring.

The Islanders football squad will lose by graduation, Looby, Criswell, Cully, Johnson and Eihl.

The Islanders won seven of eight football games played and scored 255 points to 49 for their opponents.

Rock Island High School's athletic teams would greatly miss Butler's talents on the field, the track, and the court

Chapter 4-The Panama-Pacific International Exposition

After the meet in Chicago, Solomon returned to Rock Island, where a group of Rock Island alumni solicited funds from the community to help with expenses that Butler would incur while at the Pan-Pac games. The *Rock Island Argus*, Hickey Brothers cigar stores, and other downtown businesses took donations. Close to $100 was raised. Solomon would be representing the community and the high school. After leaving Rock Island from the 5th Avenue depot, he headed west to Hutchinson, Kansas to visit his parents before leaving for the San Francisco meet in August to compete against the fastest runners in the country. While on his way to the meet, he stopped at the Shorter AME Church in Denver, Colorado, where he displayed the multitude of awards he had won over the past three years. Admission was 25 cents, and a large crowd turned out to see his hardware. The money earned here, along with the money donated by the Rock Island community, helped to offset his expenses in San Francisco.

The Shorter A.M.E. Church in Denver

SOL BUTLER IN FINAL WORKOUT

TWO WEEKS' STRENUOUS PRAC-
TICE FOR MEET ENDS TODAY

Colored Star Will Leave for San Fran-
cisco in Morning—Determined
To Win

After two weeks of the most strenuous practice preparing for the fair
meet to be held at San Francisco,
August 6 and 7, "Sol" Butler, who is
confident he will take a first place at
the big meet and place Rock Island
on the score board, will depart for the
coast tomorrow morning at 3:05
o'clock on No. 5, over the Rock Island.
He will arrive at Denver on Saturday
morning and from there he will travel
over the Southern Pacific to the
coast. "Sol" will probably be accompanied by his brother, Ben.

Butler broke the C. A. A. broad
jump record at Chicago on July
17, at the meet to select a team
from the central states. He cleared
the turn at 24 feet and 2½ inches,
which is expected to be sufficient to
cop the event at the coast meet, although Butler will be opposed by the
best university men in the country.
Sol stated this morning just before
taking his last workout that he was
confident of breaking his own record
and will do his utmost to smash the
world's record, which is a few more
inches. Entered in the broad jump
and expected to be the winner by the
dopesters, he will also participate in
the 100 and 220 yard dashes, which
events he was defeated in at Chicago,
owing to a poor start.

The Butler fund being solicited
among local high school alumni and
merchants and athletic fans to be
used in defraying the expenses of the
colored athlete at the Panama exposition athletic meet is being swelled
daily. Up until this noon over $50
has been raised and it is expected by
nightfall that it will reach the $100
mark. The high school athletic association contributed $10 towards the
fund. On his return Butler will stop
at his home in Hutchinson, Kan. and
visit his parents, returning to Rock Island about September 5.

The track meet portion of the Panama-Pacific Exposition was held on August 6-7, 1915. The entire Expo was staged to celebrate the completion of the Panama Canal, but more importantly, it highlighted San Francisco's comeback from the 1906 earthquake. Butler was one of a very few athletes from the Midwest to compete in both the junior and senior championship events. It was his first international track meet. While not a member of a track club, but representing himself and Rock Island High School, he was expected to place high in the broad jump. The *West Virginian* newspaper wrote, *"He has legs of steel springs and goes from the take-off like a shot."* At the junior competition on the 6th, Sol won the broad jump by leaping 22 feet, 11 inches.

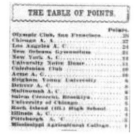

Headlines from the *Rock Island Argus* December 1915

The next day, at the senior event, Butler competed against F.G. Stiles of Wisconsin, the 1913 world champion, and Platt Adams, the Olympic champ in the broad jump. Stiles was picked to win, and Butler was heralded as a top contender. However, in the preliminaries, Sol pulled a muscle and had to withdraw. Henry Worthington of the Boston Athletic Association won with a leap of 23 feet, 10 inches, besting Stiles.

BUTLER HONORED BY 1915 REVIEW

Statistics of Chicago Tribune Names Sol In Two Instances Tying World's Records.

In the annual review of sports, computed by the Chicago Tribune, one Rock Island athlete is prominently mentioned in records for 1915. That boy is Sol Butler, colored star, who tied two world's records during the past year in meets at Chicago. At the northwestern indoor track meet Sol stepped 60 yards in :06 2-5, equalling the world's record, and on July 17, in the trials for the A. U.U. meet to be held in San Francisco, Butler did 24 feet 2½ inches in the running broad jump at Chicago, equalling the world's record. In the junior meet later at the San Francisco exposition, Butler did not set any records, but copped the running broad jump, making him a world's champion. Sol is at present attending the Dubuque German college and he was one of the shining lights on the Dubuque football team this past season.

Sol and his brother Ben are spending the holidays with friends in Rock Island.

Butler was honored by the *Chicago Tribune* for his record-setting feats while attending Rock Island High School.

By the way, Sol Butler asks us to deny the statement alleged to have been made by a New York historian in our fair city recently that his name was in the lineup of the team that played in Rome in 1200 B. C. He declares the first time he donned moleskins was after recuperating from wounds incurred in the Revolutionary war.

Sol had a tremendous sense of humor. When jokingly asked in an interview if he played football in ancient Rome, this was his response.

Daily Dispatch   November 12, 1915

OUTLOOK DARK IN EXPO. MEET; NEGROES HAVE THE CLASS IN THREE BIG EVENTS

The photos show Sol Butler, broad jumper; Howard Drew, in starting position, and Binga Dismond, runner, who will make white athletes stretch themselves in the national championship competition. Butler and Drew are tipped as sure winners.

This headline and photo of Butler appeared in newspapers across the United States.

Chapter 5-The College Years

During the summer of 1915, Solomon had set up a shoeshine business in downtown Rock Island to earn money to support himself and to hopefully enroll in college to further his education. One of his customers, Episcopal Reverend Ben Lindeman, of Bettendorf, Iowa, befriended Butler after watching him play football and track. Lindeman, a Dubuque German College and Seminary graduate, told him about the school and had him contact Coach John Chalmers. Eventually, Butler negotiated a scholarship for himself and his brother Benjamin, and they would be the first black athletic students to attend Dubuque. The Dubuque Telegraph-Herald would document his admission into college through this story, later published in 1936.

"Butler had been recommended to the 'U' coach by an alumnus as promising football material. But to the president's consternation the boy demanded that an agreement for a stipulated sum of money be signed, in recognition of his athletic ability before he should enter the college classes. "Never have I signed such a contract," the president exclaimed. "I will sign none for you." Yet, the colored boy was not at once dismissed from the room. You misunderstand the purpose of Dubuque," its president explained. "Its aim is to help students get an education, whether or not they have money to pay for it. Now, if you really want to go to college, if you have the character necessary for making an education worthwhile, but have no money, we can help you. I assure you of an education, just as I have done with other boys, but not on account of athletics. You must come to us because you want to go to college, or not at all."

"Well," the boy replied, not at all abashed, "I have an offer of one thousand dollars from a big university, and certainly ought to have enough money to pay my expenses, if I'm going to stay here." "If that is the way you feel about it, I cannot talk to you anymore. But, "the president added impressively, "if you do come to Dubuque, and if on even the first day of football practice you happen to break your leg or are

otherwise incapacitated by physical injury, you need have no fear. We will see that your injury does not make you leave college; we will continue to care for you, and pay your expenses as if you were still able to do the manual labor to which you are assigned. That's all."

"Coach and athlete left the office, but in a few minutes returned. "Well," the colored boy rather patronizingly announced, "I'll trust you!"

Sol and Ben's freshman class at Dubuque German College.   From the University of Dubuque, Charles C. Myers Library Archives

A newspaper article of the day stated that Lake Forest College in Chicago had hired Herbert Roe and that Butler was following him to participate in track. The story ended up being false.

When Butler took the field for the first time in his collegiate career as quarterback, he weighed only 167 pounds. Dubuque German College's fall season of 1915 started off on October 1 by playing Teacher's College of Cedar Falls, beating them, 25-7. Even at quarterback, Butler showed his speed by rushing for 167 yards.   The following week, Ellsworth College hosted Dubuque and lost 28-0. In this game, he scored in the first and fourth quarters. October 23 saw Dubuque travel to Campion College and beat them, 23-0. Butler scored in the second quarter after runs of 33 and 28 yards. In the first home game of the season, the University of Wisconsin-La Crosse played at Dubuque and lost 27-0. Cold weather hampered the next week's November 5 game at Upper Iowa College where Dubuque won 13-6. The team took automobiles to this game. Sol would score on a fake forward pass and ran it in for 15 yards. Before the game with St. Ambrose, Butler wrote this letter to the sports editor of the Dubuque *Telegraph-Herald*, a bit exasperated by accusations (and with a bit of tongue in cheek) that he was getting compensated for being at Dubuque German College. *"To the sporting editor of the Dubuque Telegraph-Herald--Dear Sir: I noticed in the columns of your paper from my thoughtful friends connected with the Davenport Times. I wish those friends for their kind interest that they have manifested in me for the past year or so. I had almost despaired of hearing from them since I have become connected with the Dubuque German College and Seminary, but since reading the articles of last night, I begin to feel like my old self again."* He continued, *"One statement about me being engaged for the football season is just a little erroneous and I wish to correct it by stating that I am locating here for an indefinite period of time, as I really like the people and the institution. Where I made my mistake, however, was in neglecting to consult The Times about the best place in the USA to eke out an education. For this sad mistake, I will never forgive myself because I realize that such thoughtful men as those connected with the Times are better able to advise one so young and inexperienced as myself. As for being a globe-trotter, the only excuse I can offer for this deplorable milady is that traveling tends to broaden one's views of life. I only wish my friends connected with the Times could bring themselves to see this as I do, and, for a summer vacation, I would recommend a trip to Dubuque via the Burlington or the Chicago and Milwaukee. Speaking of the term 'yanked', I have not advanced far enough in English to know whether that verb comes under the title of GOOD USAGE or not, but I hope that my more intimate friends will not misinterpret the significance of the word and think that a man like Mr. Chambers would be so cruel to YANK a young and innocent fellow like myself into such a dreadful institution as the Dubuque German College. Speaking seriously on the subject, I wish to deny that I have received any pecuniary compensation whatsoever for my athlete ability."* Signed *Sol Butler.* The boys from St. Ambrose College in Davenport traveled upriver to Dubuque, only to receive a 63-0 thrashing. In this game, Sol scored the first touchdown. On his second score, he ran up the middle after completing a spectacular 30-yard pass. He was pulled from the game in the second half after he twisted his ankle. Crosstown rival St. Joseph's College (now Loras College), was the next victim with a 13-7 loss on Thanksgiving. Butler faced Will Gleason, also a Rock Island High School graduate, as the respective quarterbacks in this game. Butler showed great leadership as he mixed up plays in advancing the ball for the first touchdown in the first quarter. Butler also handled punt returns in this game. A crowd of 6,500 fans watched the intercity rivalry. The game was so well attended, that extra bleachers were constructed. A record $4,000 in gate receipts were taken in and split evenly between the two schools. The school ended its season with a perfect 7-0 record and won the Hawkeye Conference Championship. Sol was named to the 1st team All Hawkeye Conference squad as quarterback.

A *Telegraph-Herald* newspaper interview in November 1915 quoted Coach Roe about Butler, *"He has won his place through hard work, sacrifice, and determination. He is the most reliable and conscientious of all the athletes I've worked with and in addition to being a wonderful performer, has exceptional qualities that stand for character and manhood."*

Butler also played basketball for Dubuque German College and Seminary and lettered as a freshman. The first game of the season was against Platteville Normal. For Christmas break, Butler traveled home to Hutchinson to visit his parents. While there, he entered a declamation contest in the Interstate Literary Association for colored people at the First Methodist Church on December 30, and received second place money for his speech. In next game of the season, Dubuque lost 17-15 against Lenox College. Butler played forward and scored two points and committed two fouls. The next foe again was Platteville Normal on January 14, with Normal winning 44-23. The local paper listed Butler as 'being the whole team for Dubuque.'

Traveling to Upper Iowa, the Dubuque boys lost 47-18, with Butler scoring only one basket. The February 5 game against Wartburg in Clinton, saw Dubuque win 36-18 with Butler playing guard and scoring four points. On February 12, the foe was Iowa State Teacher's College and Dubuque won, 25-24. He played guard this game and committed two fouls. On February 16 Dubuque lost to La Crosse Normal 36-24, with Butler playing guard and scored four points. Dubuque traveled to Cedar Falls on February 19, losing 44-11. The next foe was Upper Iowa and Dubuque lost 36-21. Butler did not play in these games as he was participating at a track meet in Chicago.

Butler's freshman basketball team   From University of Dubuque, Charles C. Meyers Library Archives

In February 1916, Solomon competed on the track team and would eventually become an All-American at the indoor 55-meter hurdles. He also ran in the outdoor season, participated at the Drake Relays in April, and was crowned Hawkeye Conference Champions for the outdoor season on May 27. At the relays, Butler would place first in four events, and second in two others. In the 100-yard dash, he placed first with a time of 10.5 seconds, first in the 120-yard high hurdles with a time of 17.5 seconds, first in the 220-yard low hurdles with a time of 28 seconds, first in the broad jump with a leap of 22 feet, 11 inches, (breaking the conference record) and finished second in the shot put and high jump, with a jump of five feet, four inches. A band played before and after the event, much to the pleasure of the 3000 fans present. Butler scored 26 points and won individual honors as Dubuque German College and Seminary would win the conference title with 51 ½ points, with Dubuque College placing second with 45 ¼ points, Iowa Teachers College with 16 1/2, Upper Iowa with 8 ¼, Buena Vista with 8, and Parsons College with 4 ½.

The following day, Butler was selected by his teammates as the team captain for the 1917 track season.

The Hotel Julien Dubuque was the setting for the all-sports banquet, held on June 1, 1916. The team and their guests watched films of the football games and were treated to a wonderful meal of chicken broth, olives, celery, Julien's special tenderloin, combination salad, strawberry ice cream, cake, coffee, and cheese crackers.

The Hotel Julien Dubuque

BUTLER HAS A BIRTHDAY

STAR COLORED ATHLETE IS NOW ENTITLED TO VOTE AS HE IS 21 YEARS OLD.

On March 3, 1916, his birthday, the track team at Dubuque gave Butler a silk track suit to wear at the big track events, which he was extremely proud of.   Butler participated in the Penn Relays on April 29; and placed 4th in the 100-yard dash.

DUBUQUE'S RELAY TEAM TO THE PENNSYLVANIA RELAY CARNIVAL

Butler as member of the 1916 relay team at the Penn Relays.   From the University of Dubuque, Charles C. Myers Library Archives

The VI Olympiad, scheduled to be held in Berlin, Germany in the spring of 1916, was cancelled due to the onset of World War I. Northwestern Coach Omer, a staunch supporter of Butler, tried to get on the track team, but the war nixed those plans.

Before the football season started at Dubuque, Butler made a return visit to Rock Island on September 25 to visit his high school, former teammates, and attended a scrimmage game at Reservoir Park. It was noted that he had added weight and muscle since graduating in 1915.

The 1916 Dubuque College football team   From the University of Dubuque, Charles C. Meyers Library Archives

The 1916 football season began on October 6 with a blowout win over Ellsworth College in Nutwood Park with a score of 54-0. Butler scored two touchdowns and kicked one PAT. In the first and only loss of the season, Dubuque fell to the University of Wisconsin-La Crosse 12-3 on October 14. He also played left halfback in this game which saw a lot of fumbles. Dubuque advanced the ball to the four-yard line twice, but never scored. On October 20, versus Wisconsin Platteville, Dubuque played on a cold, muddy field, covered with straw, against a stiff frigid wind, in front of 150 fans. Butler scored on a 70-yard run in the first quarter. Dubuque hosted Upper Iowa College on November 4. Butler scored three touchdowns on runs of 65, 70, and 95 yards, leading Dubuque to a 38-0 win. Butler intercepted a pass from Upper Iowa and ran 40 yards to set up another score. In the third quarter, Upper Iowa kicked off to Kirtland of Dubuque, who picked up the ball on the five-yard line. Butler came from behind, took the ball from Kirtland and raced for a 95-yard score. Traveling to Cedar Falls on November 11 to play the Iowa State Teachers College, Dubuque won by a slim margin 13-6. In the last game of the season, against Buena Vista College, the Dubuque team was victorious again 39-0. Butler scored three touchdowns in this game, one of them being a 30-yard interception to score. In the fourth quarter, he misjudged a punt, and the ball rolled into the end zone where he picked it up and ran 100 yards for a touchdown. Butler was again named to the All Hawkeye Conference first team at quarterback. In a letter to his father about this game, Butler wrote, "We are now tied with the same team we defeated last season and are trying to arrange a post season contest. If this is done, I feel sure we can annex the state title."

Butler earned his D sweater for football. From the University of Dubuque, Charles C. Meyers Library Archives

Again, during the winter months, Butler played basketball for Dubuque, which was only in its second year of existence at the school.

The 1916-17 Dubuque German College basketball team. From the University of Dubuque, Charles C. Myers Library Archives

On February 9, 1917, Butler gave a speech at the local Masonic hall on the ways of maintaining social unity among the black community. He reflected "that a clean life opened up greater avenues for the black man." The Inter-Class Indoor Meet was scheduled for March 10. Because it was an inside event, the dashes were reduced to fit the gym. Butler won the 21-yard high and low hurdles with a time of 3.15 seconds, and the 200-yard dash in 28 seconds. His brother Ben would win the 21-yard dash with a time of three seconds; and won the standing broad jump in nine feet, two inches. On April 6, the United States declared war on Germany. Many colleges across the country cancelled athletic events; and focused on military training for the men. On April 14 was the Inter-Class Outdoor Track Carnival, an event that pitted the four classes against each other in competition. Butler won the 100-yard dash with a time of 11.25 seconds, the 60-yard dash in eight seconds, and the 50-yard dash in six seconds. His brother Ben would place first in the broad jump with a leap of 16 feet, 11 ½ inches. Sol did not participate in the broad jump. With Coach Chalmers away coaching the baseball team, Butler took over the role of coach for this event. The sophomores won with 42 points, the juniors winning 35 points, the seniors getting 29 points, and the freshman finishing last with 21 points.

Traveling to Philadelphia on April 28 to participate in the 23rd annual Penn Relays, Butler scored seven points by winning first place in the broad jump with a mark of 23 feet, 5 ¾ inches and would take third place in the 100-yard dash. Over 100 colleges competed in this year's meet, which was blessed with good weather. He would also garner All-American status at this meet.

Butler, far right, finished third in the 100 yard dash at the Penn Relays   Source-*Philadelphia Inquirer*

RELAY CARNIVAL WINNERS

CHAMPIONSHIP RELAY RACES

One-mile, College—Pennsylvania. Time, 3.25 1-5.

Two-mile, College—Pennsylvania. Time, 8 2-5 seconds, equalling the Pennsylvania record made in 1911.

Four-mile, College—Chicago. Time, 18.39 1-5.

One-mile, Freshman—Pennsylvania. Time, 3.22, breaking record of 3.25 4-5 made in 1913 by the Penn team composed of Lockwood, Kelly, Bacon and Meredith.

Middle Atlantic State Collegiate A. A.—Dickinson. Time, 3.31 3-5. New event on the programme.

One-mile, High School—Newark Central. Time, 3.32 2-5.

One-mile Preparatory School—Exeter. Time, 3.29 3-5.

One-mile, Roman Catholic School—St. Benedict's, Newark, N. J. Time, 3.37 1-5.

SPECIAL EVENTS

100 Yards Dash—Brewer, Maryland State. Time, 15 2-5. Ganzmiller, of Pennsylvania State, won the event, but was disqualified, as he is under suspension by the A. A. U. His time was 10 2-5.

120 Yards Hurdles on Grass—Simpson, Missouri. Time, 15 2-5 second.

FIELD EVENTS

Pole Vault—W. Newstetter, Pennsylvania, 12 feet 6 inches.

High Jump—Larsen, Brigham Young University, 6 feet 5⅜ inches, breaking the intercollegiate record of 6 feet 4½ inches made by Oler, Yale, 1915.

Javelin Throw—Nourse, Princeton, 165 feet ¾-inch.

Shot-put—Sinclair, Princeton, 45 feet 1-inch.

Broad Jump—Butler, Dubuque, 23 feet 5¾ inches.

Discus Throw—Huster, Illinois, 128 feet 7½ inches.

Back Row—
DIRKS
WESCOTT
B. BUTLER
CHALMERS (Coach)

Front Row—
ARENDS
S. BUTLER
CORDS
C. PARKER

The 1917 Dubuque German College track team. From the University of Dubuque, Charles C. Myers Library Archives

This photo of Sol would run in newspapers across the nation

After the Penn Relays, their next track meet was a dual meet with La Crosse Normal on May 5. On a soggy track, Dubuque won with 76 ½ points over their opponents' 40 points. Butler won the 100-yard dash with a time of 10.35 seconds, placed first in the high hurdles with a time of 17.25 seconds, first in the shot put with a toss of 38 feet, 1 ½ inches, first in the broad jump with 21 feet, 3 ¾ inches, first in the 200 yard hurdles with a time of 28.45 seconds, and third in the discus. His brother Ben finished second in the 440-yard dash, after falling and nearly finishing first. During a practice after school on May 10, Butler ran the quarter mile in 54 seconds. Ben also served as a football manager and was his brother's roommate.

The big event of the season was the Hawkeye Conference Meet, held at 1:30 p.m. on May 26. Dubuque German College and Seminary won the event with 92 points, followed by Buena Vista with 36 points, and Iowa State Teachers College with 35. St. Ambrose and Lenox did not participate because they discontinued athletics at the onset of World War I. At the conference meet, Butler won the 100-yard dash with a time of just over 10 seconds, the 120-yard high hurdles in 16.5 seconds, the 220-yard dash in just over 26 seconds, and the broad jump with a hop of 22 feet, 9 ½ inches. He also placed third in the discus, second in the shot put, and fourth in the javelin. This was the first year for javelin in the conference. He also participated on the first-place half-mile relay team. Brother Ben was a runner on the first-place mile-relay team that finished with a time of 3 minutes, 56 seconds. Ben also entered the high jump and the broad jump. Sol won individual honors by scoring 26 of the team's points. The second annual sports banquet was held the following evening at Peters Commons at 6:30 p.m. The meal, prepared by Mrs. Steffens, wife of the college president, was so good, that the boys gave her an ovation that shook the rafters. On May 31, Solomon traveled to his former home in Hutchinson, Kansas and registered for the draft. He was 22 years old, and his parents still lived at 324 B Avenue West. While visiting his parents during the summer, Butler displayed his high school and college track hardware in a Hutchinson storefront window for all to see. All told, he had 137 medals, 22 silver cups, and seven shields. He had them insured for $1,500 and said he 'would not sell them for any price."

Football season arrived on September 29, 1917 and Dubuque hosted the University of Wisconsin-Platteville and pounded them in a loss of 40-0. In the first quarter, Butler took a short kick 25 yards for a touchdown and in the second quarter, completed a pass to Ansberg for another score. He also kicked four PATs in the game and was pulled in the third quarter to rest. After a week break, they again played the University of Wisconsin-La Crosse and beat them, 41-0. The following week, they beat Ellsworth by a score of 40-0. On November 3, Dubuque hosted Cornell and played to a 13-13 tie. The field was extremely muddy, yet it didn't slow Butler down. He scored a touchdown in the first quarter, missed the PAT. Later in the first, Cornell punted to Butler who advanced the ball 60 yards for another touchdown and kicked the PAT. The second quarter did not fare well for Butler as he was downed for a 12-yard loss, threw two interceptions, and completed only one pass for 20 yards. Cornell punted to Krebs in the third, and performed a crisscross pattern to Butler, who ran the ball for 50 yards.

The 1917 Dubuque German College football team. From the University of Dubuque, Charles C. Myers Library Archives

One of the highlights of Butler's college football career was playing in one of the most lopsided games in college football history. On November 16, Buena Vista College traveled from Storm Lake, Iowa to Dubuque, only to be drubbed by a score of 125-0. Butler had over 200 yards rushing, including runs of 35, 69, and 95 yards. He also completed a 100-yard punt return, much to the delight of the crowd, and scored five touchdowns and kicked all the extra points.   Buena Vista's center, Clifford Drury, was quoted after the game, *"We couldn't catch Sol Butler. On the average, they scored a touchdown every four minutes. I remember the crowd yelling, "We want a hundred." They got it and then they cried, we want another 100."* Dubuque wrapped up the 1917 season with a decisive victory of 43-0 over Upper Iowa. Once again, Butler was named to the All-Hawkeye Conference first team at quarterback.   Butler and his brother Ben were invited for Thanksgiving dinner at the home of Flem Bassett and his wife, who lived at 516-8th Street in Rock Island. The couple had befriended the Butler brothers when they lived in Rock Island.

A sideline shot of the Dubuque football team   From the University of Dubuque, Charles C. Meyers Library Archives

During one of the few baseball games Butler appeared in for Dubuque College, the team was playing St. Ambrose in Davenport, Iowa, and first baseman Butler hit a double in the first inning. Later, in the fifth inning, Butler was caught 'napping' off of second base, and the crowd teased the track star about it as he walked back to the dugout. He jawed back at the home crowd and they exploded with laughter. *(Oh to know what he said.)* St. Ambrose ended up taking the game, 10-8.

Butler on his way to another touchdown

From the University of Dubuque, Charles C. Meyers Library Archives

Sol mugging for the camera

From the University of Dubuque, Charles C. Meyers Library Archives

Sol's good nature was demonstrated by participating in a black-face minstrel show

From the University of Dubuque, Charles C. Meyers Library Archives

Sol Butler   **From the University of Dubuque, Charles C. Myers Library Archives**

Sol poses with the hardware he earned at track meets. From the University of Dubuque, Charles C. Myers Library Archives

WILL COMPETE IN DRAKE RELAYS

SOL BUTLER

HOWARD DREW

Howard Drew, champion sprinter of the world, and Sol Butler, probably the greatest all around Negro athlete ever developed in the

middlewest, will compete in the special 100-yard race, which is expected to be the feature of the 1918 Drake relay meet.

Both Drew and Butler will find the competition keen for some of the fastest men in the Mississippi valley, including Scholz of Missouri, will be entered.

Drew is the greatest 100 yard dash man in the world today, and Butler is one of the greatest all around athletes. He is a good sprinter, a wonderful broad jumper, an excellent basketball player and a star football man.

Butler participated in the Drake Relays, running in a special 100-yard dash that featured Howard Drew of Drake, Jackson Sholz of Missouri, Johnson of Michigan, and Carroll of Illinois. Drew, who could run this race in under 10 seconds and was expected to win, did not finish and Sholz won the event as it was snowing and the lanes weren't visible. Butler finished fourth.

On March 2, 1918, the Dubuque track team ventured to the second annual University of Illinois track carnival. Butler was the only member that placed, finished third in the 75-yard dash and capturing the broad jump with a leap of 22 feet, 8 ¼ inches.

Sol Butler of Dubuque Seminary First in Broad Jump and Third in Dash.

On April 28, 1918, the Dubuque German College track team traveled to La Crosse, Wisconsin to take on the La Crosse Normal College athletes. Butler was picked to win seven first places in his events, but took 'only' five firsts, and a tie for second and third. He set a new meet record in the broad jump at 21 feet, 11 ½ inches, and finished first in the 100 yard dash at 10 2-5 seconds, the 120 high hurdles at 17 2-5 seconds, the 220 low hurdles in 30 seconds, and the shot put at 37 feet, 3 inches. Dubuque won the meet 64 1-3 points to Normal's 53 2-3 points.

SOL BUTLER AND MEN HAVE NARROW ESCAPE AT NORMALS' HANDS

Butler's life wasn't about sports all the time. While on a visit to his parent's home in Hutchinson during the summer of 1918, he would participate at an emancipation celebration at Gano Ball Park. The citizens of the town and surrounding communities were invited for free barbequed meat and all the red lemonade they could drink. There were sack races, wheelbarrow races, a guess the number of beans in the jar contest, and other games, and of course, a broad jump competition where Butler would award the winner a large watermelon. He later gave an exhibition of his athletic skills.

Coach John Chalmers of Dubuque German College and Seminary

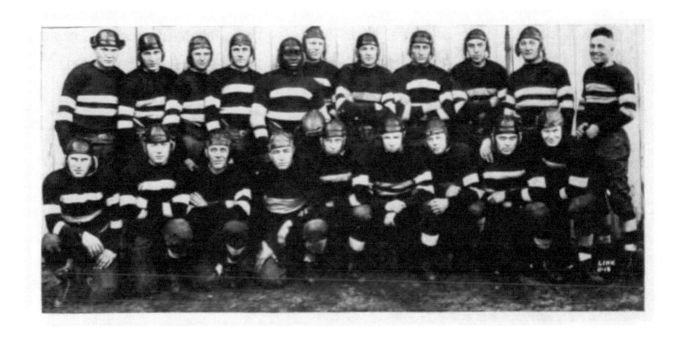

The 1918 Dubuque German College football team.   From the University of Dubuque, Charles C. Myers Library Archives

Before the start of the football season, Butler and his brother Ben sponsored a social event at the Broadus Hall in Hutchinson on September 9, 1918. Ben opened the meeting with a short talk in which he emphasized "the need for organization and competent intelligent leadership in the black race."   Butler spoke of the progress that was being made by members of the race in other communities and looked forward to that happening in Hutchinson. He stated that he was looking forward to the time when Hutchinson would afford leaders who would be trusted by members of both races, and who could raise the standing of his people. He also made the point that the ballot should be carefully utilized as an intelligent weapon, that cooperation and organization spell a brighter future, and that the race is in need of intelligent leaders. The meeting was well attended by the local black community.

The 1918 football season for Dubuque was a short one: with only three games being played due to the America's involvement in World War I. In the first game, Dubuque traveled to the University of Wisconsin-La Crosse on October 5, but lost 13-7. The next game was at Grinnell College on October 12, Dubuque won 13-0. North Central of Illinois visited Dubuque on November 16, only to be shut out by a score of 52-0.   There was no Hawkeye Conference Championship game or conference team selected. In Butler's career at Dubuque, the team produced a 19-2-1 record, and three Hawkeye Conference Championships; and for himself, three All-

Hawkeye Conference honors. Butler would complete his four year college football career with an average of 25 yards per carry, as a quarterback! This record stands today as an unofficial NCAA record.

Municipal Field in Dubuque.   From the University of Dubuque, Charles C. Myers Library Archive

Dubuque, Iowa as it would have looked when Butler lived here.

Sol as quarterback for Dubuque German College and Seminary.   From the University of Dubuque, Charles C. Myers Library Archives

The total football record for Butler for high school and college was 46-7-4. He lettered all four years in three sports at Dubuque and was team captain in track and football. He was also the first black athlete in the United States to quarterback a college team for four years.

Butler played point guard while at Dubuque and was known for his strong jumping abilities and speed on the hardwood. They garnered seven victories against five defeats in his senior year.

The 1918-19 Dubuque German College basketball team. From the University of Dubuque, Charles C. Myers Library Archives

Butler received news of his father's death and traveled back to Hutchinson to attend the funeral. Ben Butler Sr., a former slave and Civil War veteran, died on April 1, 1919, after a three month illness. After the funeral, he returned to Dubuque to finish his education and stellar track career.

Card of Thanks.
We wish to thank our many friends for the kindness shown us during the illness and death of our beloved husband, father and grandfather; and for the many beautiful floral offerings.
MRS. BENJAMIN BUTLER,
MR. AND MRS. EDWARD DOLAN,
MRS. ANNA GARDNER,
BENJAMIN F. BUTLER,
SOLOMON BUTLER,
MISS JOSEPHINE BUTLER,
VELMA MAY GARDNER,
HOWARD BUTLER.

A card of thanks was published in the Hutchinson newspaper from the Butler family.

Benjamin Butler Sr., Civil War veteran

On April 19, 1919, Butler traveled to Des Moines to run in the 10th annual Drake Relays. A stiff wind greeted the participants, where the featured event was the 100-yard dash. Carl Haas of Grinnell beat Butler by a mere six inches, with a time of 10.15 seconds. The race was so close that the judges had to announce the winner to the crowd of over 4000 fans. Butler was the anchor of the half-mile relay team that finished first place. As teammate Bergman passed the baton to Butler, South Dakota and Coe Colleges were in the lead, but as he entered the final turn, Butler blew by his opponents and won by 25 yards. Schools that participated at Drake this year were Michigan, Coe, South Dakota, Dubuque, Notre Dame, Illinois, Minnesota, Wisconsin, Grinnell, McDonough, Wabash, Hamline, Parsons, Kansas, Nebraska, Drake, Morningside, Cornell, Iowa State, Simpson, and the University of Chicago.

On April 25, 1919, with a cold northwest wind blowing at 20 miles per hour at the Penn Relays at Franklin Field in Philadelphia, Butler won the 100-yard dash in 10.35 seconds and the broad jump for the second consecutive year; this time earning All-American status for his efforts. His leap of 22 feet, 11 1/4 inches set a meet record, besting by almost nine inches the previous record set in 1915. Butler also won second place in the 200-meter run and placed sixth in the 1500-meter run, seventh in the discus with a throw of 95 feet, three inches, and ninth in the javelin with a throw of 123 feet, eight inches. He finished fourth overall with 24 points. The Penn Relays were attended by 117 colleges, 119 high schools, 57 prep schools, and 71 grammar schools.

Sol with his 22 foot, 11 ½ inch leap at the 25th Annual Penn Relays on April 25, 1919   **Source- Library of Congress**

Butler (left) wins the 100-yard dash at Penn Relays   Source- *Rock Island Argus*

On a cold spring morning on May 3, 1919, Dubuque competed at a dual meet with Coe College in Cedar Rapids, Iowa. Butler placed first in the 100-yard dash with a time of 10.02 seconds; first in the 120-yard hurdles at 17.3 seconds; first in the shot put with a toss of 37 feet, 11 inches; first in the 220-yard hurdles with a time of 27.1 seconds, first in the broad jump with a leap of 20 feet, 11 inches; second place in the discus; and third place in the javelin. He amassed a total of 32 of the team's total 52 points, but it was not quite enough to beat Coe, which won the dual meet with a total of 84 points. After this meet, Butler took the train to visit his mother and sisters in Hutchinson at 324-West 13th Street for a period of almost two weeks.

Back Row—
DIRKS
WESCOTT
B. BUTLER
CHALMERS (Coach)

Front Row—
ARENDS
S. BUTLER
CORDS
C. PARKER

The 1919 Dubuque German College track team.   From the University of Dubuque, Charles C. Myers Library Archives

At the Iowa Conference meet in Cedar Rapids on May 17, 1919, Butler set two conference records by winning the 100-yard dash in 10 seconds flat, and the broad jump with a leap of 21 feet, 6 inches. In his other events, he won the shot put with a throw of 38 feet, 7 ¾ inches; the 220-yard hurdles in 26.2 seconds; and the 220-yard dash in 22.15 seconds. Coe won the meet with a total of 53 points, Dubuque placed second with 41 points (of which Butler had 25) Simpson College with 30 ¾ points; Cornell with 25 ¾ points; Des Moines College with 14 ½ points; Parsons with six; Iowa Wesleyan with four; and William Penn's two man team zero.

During his years at Dubuque, Butler saw limited time on the baseball field since track season overlapped with baseball. During his senior year, he played first base, participated in two games, had five at-bats, scored one run, and had two hits.

The day of May 27, 1919, was set aside for the upper classmen banquet, but the freshmen were having different ideas this year. The day before, Butler had bet five of his football teammates that he would not be absent for the festivities. Yet, before breakfast, the stillness of the morning was disrupted by the clammering of automobiles, doors slamming, and chains rattling. And at the breakfast table, the senior class president George Sisler and Sol Butler were absent. A hazing was in the works and the boys were shackled and driven away.

Sol posing with his captors at the Chevrolet getaway car   From the University of Dubuque, Charles C. Myers Library Archive

Rumors persisted of happenings in Galena, Illinois, and in Epworth, and Maquoketa, Iowa. But the best laid plans sometimes have flaws in them, and word was out of their whereabouts and their schemes with the senior men. The normally peaceful town of Epworth was interrupted at 5 a.m. by the speeding of two cars to nab Sisler. At the same time, the freshmen had been spotted in a field near Kidder, Iowa, taking photos of their captives and playing cards with them. The quiet setting was soon broken by the arrival of the sophomores, who outnumbered their frosh revelers, and the seniors were rescued, only after the elders had been dunked in a pond and had muddied their clothes. The sophomores returned the captives to their banquet in their filthy and wet clothes. And it the end, it was all in the good nature of school spirit.

Sol with his captors

In the red wagon

Sol in leg irons

This series of photos courtesy of University of Dubuque, Charles C. Myers Library Archives

Solomon Butler-Class of 1919

From the University of Dubuque, Charles C. Myers Library Archives

In May, Butler completed his studies, earning a BA in History. He was also a member of the Glee Club, College Chorus, the school newspaper and yearbook, and the Philophrenic Club. He gave lectures and was invited to give the commencement speech that he had written titled, "The Negro-A Factor in the Life of America." However, he missed graduation because he was competing in the Inter-Allied Games in Paris. While at Dubuque, Butler had roomed with his brother Ben in Severance Hall and was a good student. Ben dropped out of school after his junior year. Butler often captivated his dorm mates into the late hours of the evening with his exceptional storytelling abilities and always spoke highly and respectfully of his father. Penn hurdler Harold Bannon said Sol was 'the most popular athlete to be around because of his wonderful humor and all-around good fellowship.'

Chapter 6-The Inter-Allied Games

Sol Butler served in the United States Army in the First Army for three years and would join the American contingency for the Inter-Allied Games in Paris. When he received word on May 28th, 1919, that he had been selected to participate in the games, he immediately telegrammed the New York office that he had accepted. With his telegram in hand and standing in the Dubuque *Telegraph-Herald* newspaper office, Butler was beaming ear to ear with a huge grin and was quoted as saying to a reporter, "Did I wire back? Why man, my acceptance was in the official's hand before I had fully read this message. I'm mighty tickled to get this opportunity." Upon his departure to Paris, the college band and a mass of fellow students escorted him to the train station. Butler competed under the National Amateur Athletic Union; but would wear his Dubuque track uniform while on French soil. These games were conducted as a replacement for the cancelled 1916 Olympic Games, but were only open to military service personnel throughout the world. On June 5, 1919, Butler and the team met at the NAAU offices in New York City and were shuttled in open sightseeing cars, along with a parade, to Hoboken, New Jersey to board a steamer with 47 of his fellow US teammates for Joinville, France.

The SS Great Northern that carried the American team to the Allied Games. Source- Wikipedia

Sol Butler, third row on right side, on the upper deck of the Great Northern as it leaves Hoboken, New Jersey.   Photos courtesy of National Archives

This undated photo shows Sol Butler in his Army uniform with an unidentified couple. This photo was discovered in an antique store in 2022.   **Courtesy of Brian Hallstroos**

Butler's US Army passport photo

The Inter-Allied Games were held at Pershing Stadium Paris, from June 22 through July 6, 1919. The stadium was built specifically for the games by US troops in just 3 months. Billed as the "Military Olympics", the games featured 1,500 soldier-athletes from 16 countries in 76 events in a dozen familiar sports, including "war games" such as grenade tossing and tug of war. The games were designed to provide a constructive way to channel the energy of millions of Allied soldiers who were awaiting demobilization in Europe after World War I had ended. Though not sanctioned by the International Olympic Committee, they were comparable. They were organized by the American Forces under General John J. Pershing and were financed by the YMCA. China was unable to send athletes; but provided financial support for medals and trophies. While at the games, the YMCA served the athletes over 10,000 gallons of ice cream and 200,000 gallons of lemonade; basic items that they didn't have while serving in combat. While at the games, Butler told a reporter to "tell them in the states that I will do all in my power to win the honors for my school and country."

The United States members of the Inter-Allied Games. Butler is in the third row, center

Bird, Paul	Corp.	401	
Bittel, Edward	Lt. Col.	402	Shooting pistol
Brauseu, Simon P.	Cpl.	2054	Baseball
Breck, Henry C.	Lt.	2018	Tennis singles, doubles team.,
Brennan, Matthew W.	Sgt.	936	Basketball
Bronder, Geo.	2nd Lt.	905	Javelin
Brown, L. E.	Sgt.	940	Basketball
Butler, Solomon	Pvt.	811	100 meter dash Running broad jump
Byrd, Richard L.	1st Lt.	889	Discus
Campbell, Floyd F.	1st Lt.	827	Relay medley (4 men)
Campbell, Tom	Sgt.	828	Relay 1600m. (4 men)
Campbell, Verle H.	1st Lt.	829	Relay 1600m. (4 men)
Caughey, Edgar	2nd Lt.	912	Shot put, 16-lbs.
Chamberlain, H. D.	Lt. Col.	1069	Riding mil. comp. prize jumping

Butler's name as it appeared in the official IAG program

Pershing Stadium in Paris, France

Butler won gold in the long jump with a leap of 24 feet, 9 ½ inches-- just 2 inches off the Olympic record; and placed in the 100-yard dash. His broad, infectious smile and winning attitude impressed King Nicholas of Montenegro.   The king, who was attending the games and thoroughly loved track meets, knighted Butler with the Third Order of Danilo on July 6. King Nicholas patted Butler on the back after shaking his hand, and it was reported that Butler's smile was 'ear wide'. The crowd of 30,000 gave him a standing ovation and thunderous applause.

Competing in the 100 yard dash

Butler winning the broad jump at the Inter-Allied Games

Butler was knighted by King Nicholas of Montenegro at the Inter-Allied Games on July 6, 1919

Photo courtesy of National Archives

A commemorative medal given to all athletes at the Inter-Allied Games

Butler received his broad jump medal from General John J. Pershing.   Photo courtesy of National Archives.

After the games, Butler toured Europe with the track team, visiting many of the important cities.   In an exhibition while in Europe, Butler scored two wins over rival Charlie Paddock, the first to be labeled as "the world's fastest human", and then completed his military service in the United States.   Upon returning to the states after the games, Butler planned on giving lectures about his experiences overseas.

Charlie Paddock, the world's fastest human

In the fall of 1919, Butler continued his education by taking several post-graduate classes at Dubuque College in the seminary studies. His continued desire to play football was met by joining the Dubuque American Legion team. A Thanksgiving Day game was played at Dubuque, Iowa against the Moline Indians. The day was extremely cold with the temperature at 10 degrees and the turf was covered with an inch of ice and snow, yet the boys from Dubuque prevailed with a 48-0 victory. Butler made several sensational runs in the game, which featured college teammates Johnny Armstrong and Vere Lowe. Advanced betting was made on the game, with wagers of over $3000 being made.

Butler was invited to be part of the Inter-State Athletic Meet in Kansas City, Missouri, on April 28, 1920, against Howard Drew, one of the world's fastest sprinters, in a series of exhibition dashes. This event featured several high schools and colleges from Kansas and Missouri, as well as competing grade schools from Kansas City, Missouri and Kansas City, Kansas.

Inter-State Athletic Meet

IN

Convention-Hall

Wednesday Evening, April 28, 1920.

RELAY RACES

Western University vs. Topeka Industrial Institute
Lincoln High School vs. Sumner High School.
Lawrence vs. Olathe, Kansas.
Y. M. C. A. vs. Geo. R. Smith.

1. Dashes—50-220-440 yards.
2. Run—80 yards.
3. Shot Put.
4. Hurdles—50 yards
5. High Jump.
6. Pole Vault.

Invitation to participate:

KANSAS CITY, KANSAS, GRADE SCHOOLS

vs.

KANSAS CITY, MISSOURI, GRADE SCHOOLS

1. Four lap Relays.
2. Dash—50 yards.

SOL BUTLER, of Dubuque College, Iowa, and HOWARD DREW, the World's famous Sprinter In Exhibition Dashes.

Chapter 7-The leap for the Olympics

The Olympics. The pinnacle for every amateur athlete. Butler was determined to be there. Years of training, confidence, and a closet full of accolades led up to this moment. Qualifying meets for the Olympic trials were held in a variety of cities across the United States such as Pasadena, New Orleans, Philadelphia, and Chicago. Butler traveled to New Orleans on June 26, 1920, to show the officials he was worthy of making the team. He quickly qualified by finishing third in the broad jump at Tulane Stadium, and moved on to the Olympic trials, held on the Harvard campus in Cambridge, Massachusetts on July 16-17. It was also the venue for the United States AAU Championships, in which he earned All-American status by winning the long jump and the 100-yard dash. His long jump of 24 feet, 8 inches, was an American record. (Shortly after this jump, he cleared 25 feet at a practice, but it did not count, as it was not at a sanctioned meet)

Goodbye to America. Farewell meeting at Manhattan Opera House from which the track and field, swimming, wrestling, boxing and fencing athletes marched directly to their boat

The United States Olympic Committee requested expediency in the processing of the team passports on July 19, and the following day, Butler applied for his passport. Fellow Dubuque student and friend R. Earl Johnson was a witness to Sol's passport, and by July 21, the State Department had received his application and approved it on the 27th. Butler was one of three black athletes to qualify for the Olympics. The

Olympic team was comprised of 108 track and field athletes, 45 swimmers, 24 wrestlers, 22 boxers, 20 fencers, and eight bike riders.

The USS Princess Makoita carried the US Olympic team to Belgium   Source- Wikipedia

1920 Olympic poster   Source- Wikipedia

The United States Olympic team sailed from New York City on July 26, 1920 to Antwerp, Belgium. A special cork track was installed on the deck for the track athletes to train on and a pool was installed for the swimmers.   The conditions aboard ship were less than desirable. Butler was one of the first to get seasick and it was quoted that "he smiled through it all; and has a broader grin than ever before." He was also the last to recover, and his teammates jokingly teased him that it was the soothing ukulele playing of swimmer Duke Kahanamoku from Hawaii that finally cured him. Although his teammates joked that he should take a dirigible to Europe, Butler sailed with the rest of the team. "African Golf", also known as craps, was banned while onboard the ship, but reports stated that Butler was seen with 11 sets of dice in his possession.

The first and second-class staterooms in which the athletes figured they would be staying in, had been sold to high-class executives, their wives, and families, who were attending the Olympics. The teams were left to lodge in the lower holds of the ship, which had previously been used for troop transport and for the return of bodies from World War I and still reeked of formaldehyde. Officials had been designated to have the hold sanitized due to the large number of rats being on board, but that task was never accomplished. After arriving in Europe, many of the athletes complained about the conditions, but it all fell on deaf ears. Upon arriving in Antwerp, many of those who were to be in charge of the athletes took off to visit the battlefields or left for Paris to go shopping. Lodging arrangements were not much better in Belgium, where many of the American athletes stayed in an old school building, which lacked adequate sanitation facilities and was fitted with army cots and bedding. Paddy Ryan, the American hammer thrower, angry that he had to bunk with Butler, took his hammer and dragged it through the streets of Antwerp, looking for Fred Rubian, the Olympic secretary. Upon arrival to the practice facilities, on his third attempt, Butler jumped a distance of 24 feet. ¼ inch on August 9, and was considered a shoe in for the gold medal. The Olympics were originally scheduled for Budapest, but due to war damage, they were relocated to Belgium. The opening ceremony took place on August 14, 1920 in the Olympic Stadium, with 29 nations participating in 156 events in 22 sports. King Albert I opened the games. This was the first Olympic meet to display the official flag with the five rings, the first to have the Olympic pledge read by an athlete, and the first to release doves as a symbol of world peace.

SOL BUTLER REPRESENTS U.S. IN WORLD ATHLETIC CONTEST

The 1920 United States Olympic team at the opening ceremony.

Twenty-nine athletes from 11 nations competed in the long jump, which Butler was favored to win. On August 17, in the preliminaries, on his very first jump, Butler pulled a hamstring on a leap of 21 feet, eight inches. His left leg was buried deep in the sand and it turned on him. His teammates saw this and assisted him to the locker room where trainers began rubbing down his leg. Butler, with tears streaming down his face, pleaded with Coach Moakley for another chance. With his leg heavily wrapped, he made another attempt and his leg collapsed as he writhed in pain. Butler laid on the ground, crying, all hope for an Olympic gold medal gone. The finals were held on August 18, and William Peterson of Sweden finished first with a leap of 23 feet, 5 ½ inches, with Carl Johnson on the US team placing second with a jump of 23 feet, 3 ¼ inches. Butler's preliminary jump left him in seventh place. It was later learned that Butler had pulled a muscle in his left leg while qualifying for the games in Boston. Trainer Jake Weber worked with Butler from the time of his leap of 24 feet, 8 inches at the tryouts until the day of the Olympics. American Olympic officials had pushed him to establish a new world record before the games in Antwerp, which helped cause the failure for Butler on his preliminary leap. On October 3, the Olympic team were treated to a parade down 5th Avenue in New York City and invited to a fine dinner at the Waldorf Astoria Hotel. New York City Mayor John Hylan personally expressed his sympathy to Butler. During an interview with Butler later in his adult life, he was asked if he had any regrets in his brilliant athletic career. He stated, "My failure in the Olympics."

Sol pulled a hamstring in his first attempt, effectively ending his bid for an Olympic gold medal.   Source-Wikipedia

Many of the American Olympians blamed the poor showing and lack of records on the deplorable conditions aboard ship, in Belgium, and at the training facilities at the Olympic venue. The sand in the jump pit for Butler was very loose and was not compacted, and the ring for the shot put was on loose soil and not on clay. Other critics blamed the officials at the Harvard trials for pushing him to set the record there, instead of letting him qualify and later setting the record during the Olympics. Butler was voted the most popular American athlete on the Olympic team. (*Had Butler won the gold medal, he would have been the first African-American to win an individual Olympic gold medal.*)

After the Olympics ended, a special event was scheduled on September 4 in London, England at Queen's Club. Colonel Howard Baker and B.G.D. Rudd, the British Empire representatives sent to greet the American athletes at the railroad station, at first could not pick out them out amongst the throng of people disembarking. That is, until they saw the gleaming face of the black Sol Butler and his ever present smile and sporting a panama hat, they made a dash to greet him. When they asked Butler what he would like to see first, he replied, "I wanna see Westminster Abbey; I wanna see the House of Parliament; I dunno what I don't wanna see." The British were enamored with him. The broad jump, Butler's premiere event, was tied by Brutus Hamilton of the University of Missouri and J. W. Merchant of San Francisco with a jump of 22 feet. Everett Bradley from the University of Kansas placed second with a jump of 21 feet, 11 ½ inches, and Butler took third place at 21 feet, 11 ¼ inches, even though he was still nursing a tender leg. After the meet, the Union Jack and the Stars and Stripes were flown next to each other, much to the pleasure of the thousands in attendance.

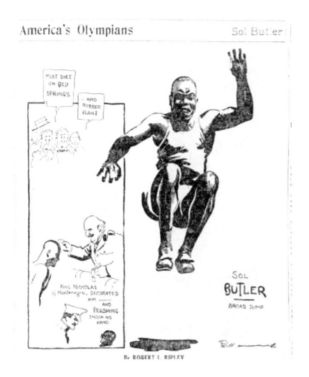

A variety of drawings depicting Sol Butler during the Inter-Allied Game and the 1920 Olympics.

Sol Butler to Study In The East

(Special to The Bystander.)

Dubuque, Iowa, Oct. 28.—Sol Butler, internationally famous colored athlete the University of Dubuque's representative to the Olympic games, doesn't intend to return to school here. Butler is in the city for a short stay before going to Hutchinson, Kans., his home. Late this month he is to give a series of instructions to members of the Chicago Athletic club, after which he will enter the Pennsylvania law school.

Butler's showing in the Olympic games was a disappointment. Regarded a sure winner in the broad jump at Antwerp, he failed even to qualify for the finals. During the preliminaries he pulled a tendon, which put him out of commission. Butler set a new world's record in the broad jump at Chicago, at the Olympic trials.

The phenomenal colored athlete was a student at the University of Dubuque for five years, during which time he not only starred on the track, but in football and basketball as well. He was one of the greatest quarterbacks ever seen in action in this part of the state.

A reported rumor about Sol leaving Dubuque for the University of Pennsylvania.

After returning to the United States, Butler went home to Kansas to visit his mother. While home, a reporter from the local newspaper asked him about the Olympics. "I don't like talking about it," he confessed. "It nearly broke my heart when that leg got hurt. I was unable to walk for several days, and was laid up for two or three weeks." Before heading east, Butler stopped at Island Park in Wichita to watch a high school football game between Wichita High and Kingman High.

The Kansas Industrial and Educational Institution, a Negro college, offered Butler the position of physical director in October 1920, but he declined. On October 22, he officiated a high school football game between two Negro schools from Wichita and Kansas City. Butler had to be the busiest athlete in the United States as he also played professional basketball for the New York Cage Five and the Chicago Forty Club. He also co-founded and played for the Chicago Savoy Five, an all-black basketball team that eventually became the Harlem Globetrotters.

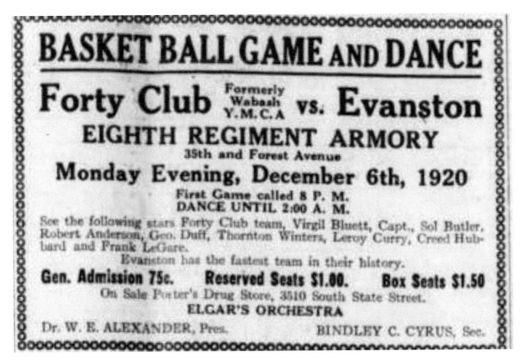

Source- The *Chicago Whip*

In 1921, Butler was honorably discharged from his duties with the United States Army.

The East Coast was Butler's next destination as he participated in the Loughlin Lyceum games at McGolrick Field at Greenpoint, Brooklyn, New York. A special sprint series was introduced at this event, with Eddie Farrell, of Fordham University, going toe to toe with Butler. In the 70, 80, and 90-yard dashes, Farrell finished first with times of 7.25 seconds, 9.25 seconds, and 9.35, with Butler right on his heels in all three events.

SOL BUTLER TWICE HIGH MAN AT MEET

Former Hutchinson Negro Track Star Holds Record At Chicago

CHICAGO, April 9.—In the 16 years that the University of Chicago's inter- scholastic track meet has been held up to its revival on May 28 next, the high point winner is Sherman Land- ers, the University of Pennsylvania star. His record of 26 points made in 1916, when at a high school at Oregon, Ill., remains the best since the meets were inaugurated in 1902.

The greatest point winners in what Coach Stagg of the University of Chi- cago calls the most national intersch- olastic track meet in the country have been these:

1902—G. M. Longshore, Grinnell, Iowa, 13 points.
1903—W. Hogenson, Lewis Institute Ac- ademy, 11 points.
1904—G. Williamson, East Division, Mil- waukee, Wis, 13 points.
1905—A. Rose, Oak Park, Ill., 10 points.
1905—L. Talbott, Kansas City Manual Training, 10 points.
1906—G. Whitman, Detroit Central High, Mich. 8 points.
1906—L. Talbott, Kansas City Manual Training, 8 points.
1906—J. C. Evans, Northwestern College Preparatory Department, Naperville, 8 points.
1906—L. V. Sampson, Petersburg, Ill., 8 points.
1907—L. Talbott, Mercersburg Academy, Pa., 15 points.
1908—L. Davenport, University Prepara- tory, Okla., 15 points.
1908—M. Alderman, Lake Forest Acad- emy, Lake Forest, Ill., 15 points.
1909—R. D. Byrd, Milford, Ill., 13 1-3 points.
1910—L. Campbell, University High School, Chicago, 10 points.
1910—M. Ingersoll, Lake Forest Academy, Lake Forest, Ill., 10 points.
1910—E. Schobinger, Harvard School, Chicago, 10 points.
1911—A. M. Mucks, Oshkosh, Wis., 11 points.
1912—C. Bachman, Englewood High, Chi- cago, 13 points.
1913—H. Goelitz, Oak Park High, Chi- cago, 13 points.
1914—S. Butler, Hutchinson, Kan., 14 points.
1915—E. Pearson, North Central High, Spokane, Washington, 13 points.
1915—S. Butler, Rock Island, Ill., 13 points.
1916—S. Landers, Oregon, Ill., 26 points.
1917—W. J. Adkins, Manteno, Ill., 12 points.

Impressive statistics for Butler at the University of Chicago Interscholastic Meet   Source-   *Wichita Eagle*

Chapter 8-The Sporting Life

The 1920's would see Butler indulge in a variety of sporting activities. In 1921, Butler had the idea of organizing and coaching a traveling female basketball team, comprised of the best black female athletes he could find. Dubbed the Chicago Roamer Girls, the women were originally affiliated with the Grace Presbyterian Church in Chicago. On March 19, 1921, they played their first game in the Eighth Regiment Armory against the Olivet Baptist Church Cosmopolitans.

The team, all natives of Louisiana, consisted of Lillian Speed, Pollie Rickman, Margrete Lewis, Virginia Willis, Corinne Robinson, Mignon Burns, Lillian Ross, Lula Porter, and the star, Isadore 'Izzy' Channels. Channels was also a world-class tennis player.

The Chicago Roamer Girls   Source: Black Fives Foundation

Butler used his experience playing high school basketball at Rock Island, at Dubuque College, and with the Chicago Savoy Five, to form the team and set a schedule with other Midwest teams. In 1925, the Roamer Girls joined the women's division of the Chicago City Basketball League and played teams all-white teams such as the Harvey Bloomers and the Taylor Trunks. They would also play against men's teams, but the men were given a handicap that they couldn't shoot any closer than the free throw line. It provided great entertainment for those who attended, and the Roamer Girls would typically beat all teams that they played, no matter the sex or color. The girls also toured Canada. They would go on to win the national title for the black women's basketball league multiple times throughout the '20s. To close the 1926 season, the Roamers defeated their arch rivals, the Olivet Cosmopolitans before a sellout crowd, in overtime with a score of 16-15, with Channels making the winning basket with a shot from half court. In the late thirties, they starred Helen 'Streamline' Smith, a 6'8" sharpshooter from LeMoyne College in Memphis, Tennessee. During their last two seasons, the Roamer Girls defeated 41 men's teams.

A poster promoting the Roamer Girls versus the Kellogg Elks

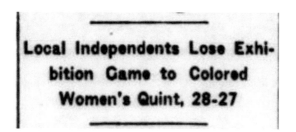

Bismarck, North Dakota *Tribune* March 1935

Sadly, the Roamer Girls and similar teams began to fold in the late 1930's.

While living in New York City during the early part of 1922, Butler took on the job of becoming a salesman at the Mahnud Auto Sales Company, one of the largest Ford dealerships in the New York City metropolitan area. He was the only black salesman and did quite well in the business.   In his first two weeks on the job, Butler had sold two cars.

A minor controversy entered Butler's life in the summer of 1922 when Butler and other athletes were called in to the Amateur Athletic Union office in New York City. The Allegheny Mountain Association filed a claim that Butler had participated in a professional basketball game in Pittsburgh a year prior.   Butler openedlly admitted the infraction and had already served a 60-day suspension.

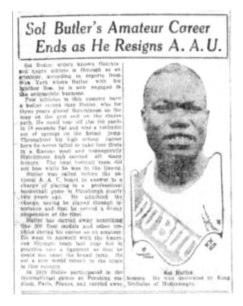

Butler resigns from the AAU, ending his amateur status as an athlete.   Source- *New York Daily News*

The New York State American Legion Games were held in Syracuse, New York in the stately Archbold Stadium on September 22, 1922, with General Pershing acting as the honorary referee.   The games hosted dozens of American Legion athletes as over 10,000 fans cheered on.   A special event at the meet was the race between Olympian Allan Woodring and a race horse.   Woodring won the 75-yard race by a foot in 7 1-5 seconds

United States Army veteran Butler, running under the flag of the Colonel Charles Young Post in New York, finished first in the running broad jump with a leap of 21 feet, 5 inches and placed third in the 100 yard dash. Winners at this event would go on the American Legion Championships to be held in New Orleans, Louisiana on October 18, 1922. Unfortunately, segregation would wind its way into Butler's life at this meet. Butler would not be allowed to compete because of the refusal of southern athletes to run against anyone except whites. Arguments were made by Legion officials that the only eligibility rules were that entrants be amateurs and members in good standing of the American Legion. Butler fit the requirements. When the New York delegation arrived in New Orleans, they escorted Butler to the finest hotel in the city, yet when they went to enter the elevator, the operator refused to move the car when he saw Butler. The New York men, led by Major Deegan, took control of the elevator and ran it to their floor. And, the night before the meet, a local committee met with the sole purpose of protesting the entry of Butler and demanded that he withdraw from competition due to the color of his skin. Southern officials stated "it would be folly for Butler to attempt to practice and suicide for him to attempt to compete." A member of the committee, Ray Murphy from Ida Grove, Iowa, took a stand that Butler be allowed to compete, since he fit the necessary criteria. In an interview in later years, Murphy recalled the moment. "I did not transmit information of this demand to Butler, but I am quite sure someone else did. He appeared at the starting point for the 100-yard dash and a bad last, as I recall." Murphy continued, "I was not at the starting point so do not know whether an occurrence took place there, similar to that which took place at the broad jump. That event took place right in front of the stands and I was directly present. Along the line of approach to the jumping block and along the side and end of the jumping pit were lined up a group of men in considerable number who had nothing to do with the track meet other, I am sure, than to intimidate Sol Butler." "Sol made a few feeble attempts and I do not believe he jumped better than 17 ½ feet, when of course he was capable of doing better than 24 feet." "I believe he took last in this event also. I would say the appearance of the observers along the line was menacing, and undoubtedly Sol decided that he had better not win the event."

Another account of this event, reported by the *St. Louis Argus*, stated that Butler was directed to perform the long jump behind a barn, away from the eyes of the predominately white crowd. At this time, there were only four Southern states that allowed black ex-servicemen in their American Legion posts- Florida, Arkansas, Tennessee, and Virginia. Many states would not allow blacks to join at all or even organize their own posts.

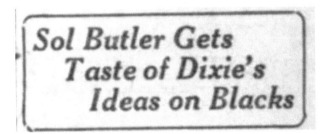

Sol Butler Gets Taste of Dixie's Ideas on Blacks

American Legion Ignored Resolution to Admit Negro

Gallant Fight By Colored Legionnaires Failed–Track Meet Management Barred Butler From Track Against New York Protests

Celebrity endorsements are nothing new. Butler endorsed these bitters back in 1922. Source-*New York Age*

Butler, still longing to be in the athletic arena, took a new course of action: professional basketball. During the early months of 1923, he founded and played for the New York Netters and traveled the country, playing other black teams such as the Indianapolis Ledger Big Five. He also played for the Chicago Defenders, and were at one time, the defending world's colored basketball champions.

FAST COLORED TEAMS PLAY

Aside from track, football was Butler's other love, and the allure of professional football called Butler. The NFL, still in its infancy, seemed appealing but the sport was primarily a white man's game and there were very few black players.

Ten minutes before the Rock Island Independents were to face off against the Chicago Bears on September 30, 1923, a solitary figure walked onto the field at Douglas Park. It was Solomon Butler. He had been watching his old high school team play against the alumni team on the field that he was about to make his debut into the NFL. He was very familiar with this venue; having played his senior year of high school football here with Rock Island High School nine years before.

The Independents had just signed Butler, who had literally no practice with the team. Earlier in the week, the *Rock Island Argus* boasted of the Independents signing numerous new players to the team, but not a word was mentioned about Butler. As he headed to the Indie sideline, the crowd of over 3500 fans stood on its feet and cheered. With the addition of Butler, was this the year that the Green and White would defeat the Bears? Also recently added to the lineup were quarterback Johnny Armstrong and R.V. Lowe, both of whom played with Butler at Dubuque College. Armstrong also played high school football with Butler in Kansas. Expectations were high for this game, since Chicago had beaten Rock Island in the past three meetings. Interestingly, the team owner had just received brand new jerseys from the sporting goods company, yet when they opened the boxes, the traditional green and white jerseys were nowhere to be seen. The company had sent red and black jerseys. The team scrambled to round up the old jerseys to be worn, since everyone knew the Rock Island team by their traditional green and white scheme.

The game began on an extremely soggy field with overcast skies, and the two teams battled back and forth in the first quarter with neither team gaining ground. Butler came into the game midway through the second quarter, and his first time touching the ball resulted in a fumble for a six-yard loss. A pass by Armstrong to Butler on the next play was incomplete, and the Indies punted to the Bears, with the ball landing in the end zone. The Bears ran one play for one yard and on the next play, Butler intercepted an Edward "Dutch" Sternaman pass on the 39-yard line. Butler ran the next play and was dropped for a two-yard loss. On the next play, Armstrong lost five yards, then completed a forward pass to Butler, who carried the ball to the Bears 27-yard line. Another pass to Butler yielded no gain. The Bears were penalized 15 yards for unnecessary roughness against Butler, this moved the ball to the 12-yard line.

Would they pass to Butler again, or run him around the end? Team Captain Herb Sies, who was the right guard and kicker, called for the ball and place kicked it through the uprights. Rock Island 3, Chicago 0 at half time.

Both teams struggled to gain momentum in the third quarter with no scoring opportunities. Butler re-entered the game in the fourth quarter, again he was handed the ball, but he fumbled it. He recovered the ball, dodged several Bear defenders, and produced a 31-yard run for a 16-yard gain. Several plays later, as Rock Island was advancing the ball down the field, Armstrong handed off to Butler, who was dropped for a five-yard loss.

The game pitched back and forth until the gun fired, signaling the end. Rock Island had beaten the mighty Chicago Bears 3-0. Not making excuses for his team, Sies stated that beside the wet conditions, Butler hadn't been given any time to learn their signals, possibly accounting for his several fumbles.

The *Chicago Tribune* was quoted as saying the Independents "sprang a surprise" by inserting Butler into the backfield.

Rock Island's Douglas Park-Home of the Rock Island Independents   Source- *Watch Tower* yearbook

Independents Batter Famous Bears, 3 to 0

SIES' PLACE KICK, FOLLOWING
15-YARD PENALTY ON BRUINS,
BRINGS WIN IN WICKED BATTLE

Butler and Armstrong Show Too Much Speed to
Heavy Chicagoans for Initial Rock Island Victory in Fourth Year of Bitter Fighting.

Rock Island wins over the Chicago Bears   Source- *Rock Island Argus*

The following week, the Cleveland Tigers visited Douglas Park to face the Rock Island Independents. Prior to the game, a representative from the Spalding Sports Company outfitted Butler with a new pair of shoes. "Now, watch 'ma speed", Butler was quoted as saying. The Tigers were a brand-new team this year and would prove to be a formidable foe. Before a crowd of 3500 fans, Armstrong resorted to a significant number of forward passes, but the Tiger defenders were always at hand to stop any scoring efforts. Butler entered the game in the third quarter, received a punt for no gain, had two runs of four and six yards over the left tackle, and played quarterback for a handful of plays. He had an incomplete pass, a fumble, and two passes for two and five yards.

The fourth quarter saw more defense from both teams, with most of the plays occurring at midfield. During the fourth period, Butler had a one-yard run, a run for no gain, and a 13-yard fumble. He was pulled from the game. The score at the end was Rock Island 0, Cleveland 0.

Duke Slater was a Rock Island Independent and the first black lineman in the NFL, and Bobby Marshall, one of the first blacks in the NFL, were both teammates of Butler's at Rock Island.

The Rochester Jeffersons visited the Indies on October 14, 1923 at Douglas Park before a crowd of 2500 fans. Although the home team blanked the visitors 56-0, it was a see-saw battle throughout most of the game. Butler's game contributions were in the second quarter, when he received a punt at the 45-yard line and zigzagged his way to the 30. In the third quarter, he had a seven-yard run off the left end, a two-yard loss behind the line, and a run for no gain.

A cool, crisp Sunday afternoon greeted the Hibbing Miners to Douglas Park on October 23, 1923. The long train ride from Minnesota must have taken its toll on the Miners as the Independents dominated the game and won 27-7. Butler did not play until the fourth quarter and contributed a 10-yard run, but it was called back on a 15-yard penalty. A run for no gain and a five-yard run were all he could muster for the cause.

A 280-mile journey to Nebraska took the Independents to face the Omaha Olympics on October 28, 1923. In the first quarter, Butler had a five-yard run over left tackle and a two-yard run up the middle. During the second period, a loss of one-yard on an end run, a three-yard run around the left end, and a 10-yard punt return were his contributions for the team. The third quarter saw him finish with a 10-yard pass reception and a nine-yard run. The Independents would beat the Olympics 22-6.

DUKE SLATER AND SOL BUTLER AT LEAGUE PARK SUNDAY, OCT. 28.

On October 31, 1923, Rock Island Athletic Association's managing secretary, J.J. Himmerman released Butler from his contract with the Independents. Butler had asked for the release so he could travel to Chicago to take over duties in a clothing store he owned with a business partner, who had fallen ill. While playing with the Independents, Butler never lived in Rock Island, but would commute by train every weekend in order to tend to his Chicago-based business.

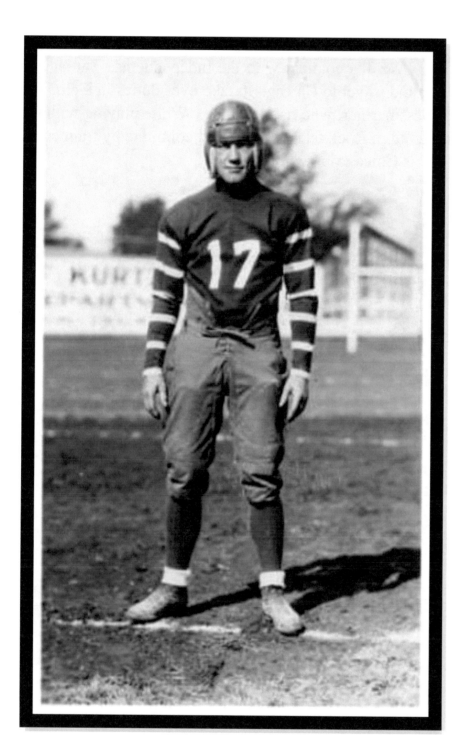

Johnny Armstrong was a life-long friend of Butler. They attended high school together in Kansas, and college in Dubuque. They would play together on the Rock Island Independents football team and eventually against each other as they moved around to different teams.

This is Armstrong as an Independent player in 1923.

Sol with Hammond Pros

This photo of Butler was taken after he joined the Hammond Pros, after his release from the Rock Island Independents football team.

Butler signed with the Hammond Pros for $10,000 shortly after leaving Rock Island and played in the last three games of the season with them. He also played five games with the Pros in 1924 as a right halfback. On October 12, 1924, the Hammond Pros visited the Rock Island Independents at Douglas Park for a 3 p.m. contest. The crowd of over 3000 fans, sitting in the wooden grandstands on an extremely hot day, saw fan favorite Sol Butler and Ink Williams play to a 24-0 loss against the Indies.

Sol Butler Coming With Hammond Team

Ink Williams

In the first quarter, Jim Thorpe punted to Butler, who ended up fumbling the ball at the Hammond seven-yard line. Two plays later, Thorpe scored the first touchdown.

Butler wanted to compete in the 1924 Olympics in Paris, but due to his affiliation with professional football, he had lost his amateur status.

Butler then relocated to the Toronto, Ohio Tigers team, a semi-pro team and later played for the Steubenville, Ohio Pros. He garnered little success with these teams. While still under contract with Hammond, Butler was contacted by Hammond's manager Doc Young to play in an all-star game, to be held at Rock Island's Douglas Park on November 8 against the mighty Independents. Fellow players Ink Williams and Bill Gardner were invited to play as well. George Johnson, manager of the Indies, and Doc Young, were bitter rivals and plenty of hype was given to the game.

Toronto Tigers Win Title by Trouncing Steubenville, 26-0

Galaxy of Former College Stars for Losers Unable to Stop Titleholders—Seeds' 90-Yard Run for Touchdown Stands Out—Hogan Kicks Pair of Field Goals.

[Special Telegram to The Gazette Times.]

STEUBENVILLE, O., Dec. 7.—The Toronto Tigers defeated the American Legion pros, 26 to 0, in the fourth and deciding game of their annual series here this afternoon, giving the Tigers the championship of the Ohio Valley and Western Pennsylvania.

The Tigers scored in the first quarter when Seeds intercepted a forward pass and ran 90 yards and over the goal line. Sol Butler of the Chicago Bears scored in the third period when he caught a forward pass from Hogan and ran 50 yards. Smith scored a touchdown in the same period after catching a forward pass from Hogan. Hogan added extra points by two good drop kicks. In the final period he kicked two field

goals. Butler, Seeds and Hogan were the stars for the winners. The lineup:

Tigers—26		Steubenville—0
Smith	L.E.	Hill
Sprinkle	L.T.	Edgar
Barry	L.G.	Setron
McRoberts	C.	Fuzzy
Secrest	R.G.	Sack
Kyle	R.T.	Keck
Nesser	R.E.	Carroll
Hogan	Q.	Bowers
Seeds	L.H.	Nardacci
Corner	R.H.	Simons
Butler	F.	Haddon

Substitutions—Browning for Sacks, Quarels for Bowers, Flannagan for Quarels. Touchdowns—Seeds, Butler, Smith. Field goals—Hogan 2. Goals after touchdowns—Hogan 2. Referee—Durfee. Williams. Umpire—Robb, Ohio State. Head linesman—Boland, Ohio State.

BUTLER SCORES IN 7-0 VICTORY OVER HAMMOND

Former Rock Island High School Star Leads Toronto To Win Over Old Teammates.

Toronto, Ohio, Oct. 5—Sol Butler, the dusky gridiron performer, was mainly responsible for the 7 to 0 defeat handed to the Hammond, Ind., professional league football team here yesterday afternoon by the Toronto Tigers, a non-league aggregation.

The touchdown was made in the first quarter by Butler, who was playing halfback for Toronto, on a 35-yard run after catching a punt. Hogan, quarterback, kicked goal. The victory was especially pleasing to Butler as he played with the Hammond eleven last season. The game was a hard fought contest, witnessed by more than 2,000 spectators.

Butler made another spectacular run in the final period when he intercepted a forward pass. Hammond was completely outplayed by the Toronto team.

All-star players from Duluth, Kenosha, Hammond, and Cleveland were invited to play in Rock Island. For reasons unknown, the game never materialized, and the Indies rescheduled a game the following week with the Kansas City Cowboys.

Butler tried his arm at professional baseball, and in 1925 at the age of 30, signed with the Kansas City Monarchs of the Negro Baseball League. Records show he pitched in only one game for seven innings, giving up six hits, one run, eight walks, and one strikeout. He had three at bats in this game.

On September 14, 1925, Butler signed with the Canton Bulldogs, showing up for practice at 185 pounds and completed the 25-man roster. A big matchup between Canton and the Columbus Tigers was staged on September 27 at Lakeview Stadium. Canton showed a weak offensive line, but their defense stood strong against the Tigers. Pete Burnum intercepted a pass from Columbus' quarterback and ran the ball back 100 yards for a score. Butler played well in the backfield, playing in the second half. He returned three punts and put Canton in position to score, but that never materialized. In the fourth quarter, Butler's return of Reichel's punt at the ten-yard line, moved the ball to the 50, and late in the fourth, Butler returned another punt from the 38-yard line to the Columbus' 39. The final score had Canton on top 14-2.

Lakeview Stadium in Canton, Ohio

The Louisville Brecks came to town on October 4, with Canton coming out on the plus side 14-0. Canton held Louisville to only one first down, and Canton produced four first downs in the first quarter, three in the second, and four in the third. Canton was four for 14 in passing with 66 yards completed. Butler completed a 15-yard pass and an 8-yard pass in the third quarter. Jim Thorpe had just signed to play with Canton a couple days before this game, and it was the first game of the season for the veteran player. Thorpe would score both touchdowns in this game. Sol Butler had won a place in the Canton's fans hearts with his ever-present smile and smooth demeanor, and even more so when he completed a forward pass to Thorpe for a touchdown after being nearly sacked for an 18-yard loss.

A significantly historic game was played on October 10, 1926 as Fritz Pollard, the first black quarterback in the NFL, played against the second black quarterback in the NFL, Solomon Butler. *(This type of quarterback pairing would not be replayed until decades later.)* Pollard played with the Akron Indians, while Butler played for the Canton Bulldogs. Butler had just been moved from running back to quarterback that week. Newspaper accounts of the day spoke of the significance of the game as the two greatest Negro athletes who had donned cleats and helmets clashed that day. Of the interest was whether "the Negro from the East or the Negro from the West stands out as the shining light." The epic matchup turned out to be a battle on the line, with Butler completing only two passes out of 11 attempts for eight yards; and had two runs for eight yards. Several missed field goals, and a defensive stand on both sides, resulted in a 0-0 tie. Canton would only produce three first downs, while Akron managed only two. Punt returns by Butler were miserable due to the strong winds that battered the field that day. Canton was penalized only 10 yards, while Akron was knocked for 30 yards. Sadly, this was the beginning of the end for black quarterbacks as Pollard was dropped from the team the following day by Akron management for a "more aggressive" game plan.

Fritz Pollard, first black quarterback in NFL and later the first black coach. Source- Wikipedia

A game of firsts

Maybe It's a Moral Victory

CANTON—0	POS.	AKRON—0
Little Twig (Carlisle)	L. E.	Daum (Akron)
Nichols (Ohio State)	L. T.	Caldwell (Wabash)
Wallace (Virginia)	L. G.	Seidelson (Pitt)
Kyle (Texas)	C.	Berry (Beloit)
Flattery (Wooster)	R. G.	McComb (Haskell)
Henry (W. & J.)	R. T.	Casey (Haskell)
Stein (W. & J.)	R. E.	Bissell (Fordham)
Butler (Dubuque)	Q. B.	Pollard (Brown)
Marker (Washington)	L. H.	Griggs (Butler)
Roderick (Columbia)	R. H.	Ursella (Minnesota)
Calac (Carlisle)	F. B.	Cramer (Hamline)

Substitutions: Canton—Speck (Canton) for Wallace, Robb (Penn State) for Marker, Marker for Calac, Thorpe (Carlisle) for Marker, Marker for Little Twig; Akron—Rohleder (Wittenberg) for Caldwell, Caldwell for Rohleder, Wendler (Ohio State) for Pollard; Newman (Carnegie Tech) for Griggs, Griggs for Ursella.

Referee—Karsh (Ohio State). Umpire—Parrett (Case). Headlinesman—Clark (Kenyon).

The lineup for the Canton-Akron game between the first and second black quarterbacks to start against each other.

On Tuesday, November 2, 1926, one of the most blatant travesties in the history of professional sports occurred. The Canton Bulldogs, with the ever-popular Jim Thorpe at halfback, took the field at the Polo Grounds to face the home team New York Giants before 40,000 fans, the most to ever witness an NFL game at that time. When the Bulldogs stepped onto the turf, Giants team owner Tim Mara and four of the Giants players, led by Cowboy Hill and three others who had attended colleges in the South, noticed that Butler, wearing number 7 and now weighing 185 pounds at 31 years old, was the quarterback and they refused to play against a black. The Giants stated that 'the crowd' may object to Butler being on the field. Doc Alexander, coach of the Giants, stated that "I am afraid Butler might get 'hurt' and cause a riot." Yet, earlier in the day, a high school game had been placed at the Polo Grounds with a school that featured three black athletes. Racially charged chants were heard from the stands, and after a 10-minute delay, Butler graciously removed himself from the game on the advice of his coach, Pete Henry, since he didn't want to disappoint the fans. The game ended in a 7-7 tie. No mention in any newspaper sports section recorded the racial incident, other than the details of the game. Decades later, *Sports Illustrated* magazine made a small mention of the game in an October 2009 story.

In 1926, when the Canton Bulldogs visited the Polo Grounds to take on the New York Giants, and Giants players refused to share the field with Canton's black running back, Sol Butler, owner Tim Mara stood with his players, forcing Butler to resolve the impasse by agreeing to sit the game out.

Had Allen 'Century' Milstead, former Rock Island High School graduate and Yale All-American, not left the Giant's team prior to this game, these two greats could have played against each other, had Butler stayed in the game.

JIM THORPE (Halfback)   SOL BUTLER (Quarterback)   Wm. FLATTERY (Guard)   BEN RODERICK (Halfback)

Butler with the Canton Bulldogs Source- *Canton Repository*

BULL DOGS TIE GIANTS, 7 TO 7

New York, Nov. 3.—Canton Bull Dogs and the New York Giants played to a 7-7 tie on the Polo grounds here yesterday. A crowd of 45,000 watched the game.

"Hinkey" Haines was the outstanding performer of the game. He gained more yardage than any other player, and scored the lone touchdown made by his team.

This is the only write up on the Canton/Giants football game from the *Rock Island Argus*. No mention was made of the Giants' refusal to play against Butler.

An article from the November 6, 1926 *Pittsburg Courier* newspaper perfectly sums up the status of how the game of football should be viewed.

The Indian—The Negro

Jim Thorpe the Indian, and Sol Butler the Negro, two of the greatest warriors who ever let slip beneath their cleated feet the white chalklines of an autumn cooled gridiron, are playing on the same team.

And everywhere these two men are being hailed in professional gridiron circles as two of the best. In fact, they are proving a real drawing card on the team from a town in Ohio which sports their names.

A white man's game—football has been called—but the white refers to the spirit of competition and supremeness in their chosen field of athletics—and not to the texture of their skin. We can't fail to marvel, however, at the fact of this Indian and this Negro, both construed by historians as belonging to a darker race, usurping the public spotlight.

Butler as quarterback with the Canton Bulldogs

Butler's last game with Canton took place at the Hartford, Connecticut Velodrome versus the Blues on November 5. An interesting set of circumstances occurred before the game. The game was to have started at 2:45 p.m., but started much later so that fans could watch or participate in the Armistice Day parade. The Bulldogs bus was eventually caught up in traffic and was late to the stadium, and when the bus arrived, the team was hustled out onto the field. The crowd of 5,000 fans saw a spectacular game with a host of forward passes and line to line stands. Stan Robb of Canton had just tackled a Hartford player when Blues' Ralph Nichols took exception and threw a punch at Robb. A multitude of punches were thrown and the police intervened. Darkness was falling and referee Holloran wanted to call the game. While Hartford scored their touchdowns in the light, Canton's score was questioned since it was getting dark and the crowd couldn't see Robb cross the goal line. The two teams met at midfield and the lights were eventually turned on. But the glare from the lights caused two offside kicks. After an exchange of the ball, Canton's quarterback took his headgear off and placed it under his arm and headed down the field, while Robb circled wide to the outside with the ball until Hartford realized what was going on and stopped him at the 20 yard line. The referee did not know what to make of this and called the game for good. The Blues won the game 16-7.

Darkness Ends Canton Bulldogs-Blues Game With Hartford In Front 16-7

The last professional team Butler would face were the Hartford Blues.

On November 13, 1926, Butler and three other players were released from the Bulldogs by Canton's management; stating that the players failed to give their best or failed enough to warrant retention. At the end of the 1926 season, Butler's former team, the Hammond Pros, had lost all four of their scheduled games and would be one of many teams to be removed from the NFL. While the Pros were never contenders in the NFL, at one time they could boast that five of the ten black players in the league's early years had played on the team, including the future Hall of Famer Fritz Pollard. The Canton Bulldogs, although winning two championships and being one of the league's first teams, was also one of Butler's teams that would be cut from the league's roster.

By the end of the 1926 season, Butler's professional football career was over. He had played for the Rock Island Independents, Hammond Pros, Akron Indians, and the Canton Bulldogs, and amassed a record of 12-33-8. He ran for 92 yards on 31 carries and scored two touchdowns; and caught nine passes for 69 yards. As quarterback, Butler attempted 14 passes, completed six passes for 57 yards with two interceptions. As a punt returner, he gathered six punts for 114 yards. While these are not great statistics by today's standards, Butler helped set a precedence by becoming one of the first black athletes in the NFL. By the start of the 1927 season, the NFL had been scaled back to 10 teams. Many of the smaller cities lost their teams due to low attendance and dwindling revenue.

Bachelor life ended for Butler when, on May 18, 1927, he married Miss Bernice Pegge, whom he met while working as the sports editor for the *Chicago Bee*.

Clinton Independents Play American Colored Giants Here Sunday

Butler would also play football for the American Giants, a Chicago team of black ex-college players who would travel the Midwest. On October 2, 1927, Butler, along with Fritz Pollard, Ink Williams, played in Clinton, Iowa against a team of locals. Reporters stated that Butler, despite his advanced age and a pronounced paunch, showed extreme nimbleness on the field and was a hard man to take off his feet.

SOL BUTLER'S "PRO" ELEVEN WINS IN IOWA

4,000 Fans Witness 7 To 0 Triumph Of All-Colored Eleven Over Clinton, Ia. Squad

ROCK ISLAND, Ill., Oct. 8.—The great Sol Butler was the Sol Butler of old when he led his American Giants, all-colored professional football team to a brilliant 7 to 0 victory over the Clinton, Ia., professional eleven at Clinton, Ia., Sunday. About 4000 fans witnessed the contest.

Both teams put up a stubborn battle. The lines withstood all assaults until the final quarter, when the Giants pulled a whirlwind finish.

In the fourth quarter Sol Butler, Dick Hudson and Doll made long gains on heavy line plunging and fast end runs.

Both teams resorted to tricky plays a great deal with little avail.

The following week, the Clinton independent team would travel to Chicago to take on the Giants again. Butler would play quarterback and score the only touchdown of the game, late in the third quarter, on an end run from the five yard line.

Chapter 9-In a Blaze of Glory

Butler's name recognition took him down a different road as he became friends with the famous black director, Oscar Micheaux, a fellow Kansasite. Micheaux ran the Lincoln Motion Picture Company, and he acted in 44 movies while in Hollywood and in Chicago. He also had several uncredited roles in Johnny Weissmuller's "Tarzan" films and in several Mae West movies.

Butler appeared in Mae West's 1935 movie, "Goin' to Town"   Source-Paramount Pictures

Yet, while he enjoyed these minor roles in films, he never gave up his love of sports and continued playing on football and basketball teams, barnstorming across the United States. Butler had to have known the nation's railroad schedule better than anyone.

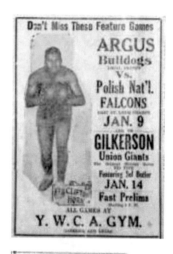

SOL BUTLER'S "PRO" ELEVEN WINS IN IOWA

4,000 Fans Witness 7 To 0 Triumph Of All-Colored Eleven Over Clinton, Ia. Squad

BLACKHAWK GRID SQUAD WINS, 20-6

West Coast All-Stars Bow to Strong Colored Eleven at White Sox Park

On December 19, 1931, Butler played with the Blackhawks football team at White Sox Park in Los Angeles and then several days later, he would be playing basketball for the Gilkerson Union Giants in the small Iowa town of Lone Tree.

Lone Tree to Play Colored Team Dec. 25

Gilkerson's Union Giants Basketball Quintet to Meet Lone Tree Indees.

On August 7, 1932, Butler purchased the former nightclub, The Showboat, once owned by the world's heavyweight boxing great Jack Johnson. It was located in the Dunbar Hotel, a hot spot for black residents on Central Avenue in Los Angeles. Butler renamed it The Harlem Showboat, with the support of a few wealthy men, plus his own backing. The club did well until October when Butler sold it to another investor.

In 1932, Butler loaned his athletic training services to Eddie Tolan, the great University of Michigan track star. Tolan, dubbed "The Midnight Express," went on to earn two gold medals in the 1932 Olympics in the 100 and 200 meter races.

During the last week of May 1933, Butler's wife, Bernice, charged that "King" Solomon Butler has done a 'broad jump' out of existence, and entered a petition for divorce. According to sources, Butler, along with fellow athlete Fritz Pollard and other baseball players, left Chicago two years ago for a series of games, but has never returned.

Butler played the lead role of Othello in a production in the Los Angeles area in 1934, after the lead removed himself due to another commitment. On his 37th birthday, Butler spend the evening playing basketball in a fraternity series in the Los Angeles area and was reported to be filled with all the 'vim and vigor' of his younger opponents.

Due to his friendship with Russell Saunders, a director and former college football player, Butler was contacted about playing a part in a new movie, Black Hell. The movie dealt with a fictional coal mining community in Pennsylvania, and the turmoil resulting from a walkout of the miners and the subsequent death of one of their leaders. Paul Muni, (of the original Scarface fame), played Joe Radek, and Butler played Mose, his working companion. The movie was renamed Black Fury before its release on May 18, 1935 and was critically acclaimed.

Black Fury movie poster and still shot from the movie. Source- Wikipedia

A letter to the sports editor of the Los Angeles Daily News on July 25, 1935, revealed Butler's take on the history of the colored American athletes rise in track and field.

"Dear Mr. Cronin: It has been brought to my attention a number of times the reasons for the colored Americans' success as broad-jumpers and sprinters. Some of the noted physicians and coaches have attributed the sensational work to the different build of the colored lad, etc. I wonder if you would be willing to take the real reason from one of the first broad-jumpers that started the parade of colored stars forward. When I first started in track it did not occur to me that someday I would be the world's champion in the event. I had my eyes fashioned on the 100-yard dash and speed became one Howard Drew was blazing the trail along that path. My coach, Don Yeoman of Hutchinson High School, Kansas, knew that I was a broad-jumper, because he had watched me in the grade school meets. I wanted to sprint and nothing else. He talked to me about pride of school and points that I would pick up in the event and so I had started broad-jumping just as a sideline. On I went through my high school career, and in the tryouts for the Panama Pacific meet at Frisco in 1915, I had a leap of 24 feet, 2 ½ inches, considered remarkable at that time, for 24-foot broad-jumpers were just as scarce then as 26-foot broad-jumpers are at the present day.

From that day started the parade of jumpers. Ned Gourdin of Harvard took up where I left off, and at Boston in 1920, Hunter Johnson, then trainer at Pitt University, came to me and told me that there was a colored lad out in his section who sent word that someday he would defeat me. I had just set a new American record of 24 feet, 8 inches and laughed at the idea. But the idle boast of Hubbard's came to be a reality at Neward, New Jersey three years later. From Hubbard the list runs to Silvo Cato of Haiti, Ed Gordon of Iowa, Jesse Owens and Eulace Peacock. And as long as these boys keep up the good work and their names are heralded on the sports sheets the world over, some dark-skinned lad will be trying to emulate his ideals.

Another example that will bear out my statement is the fact that when Binga Desmond, great quarter-miler of Chicago University, was running world's record time in the event, we had more colored quarter-milers during his era than ever before or since. With Desmond as tops, well, a brother, at Syracuse; Motley of Colgate; Howe, once a sprinter during Drew's time, turned quarter-miler, and he hailed from Colby; Dewey Rogers of Penn, and Cecil Cooke of Syracuse. These boys trained on after Desmond, their ideal, and with the passing of Cooke and the introduction of Eddie Tolan and Metcalfe, the colored youth's ideals went back to the makers of speed.

There is an old saying in track, 'That no profit come wherein no pleasure taken', and that is the reason. No different build, as all of the men I have mentioned have varied in builds as easily as their names have varied. I was a type that looked like a weight man, Hubbard was lithe and rangy. Ned Gourdin and Ed Gordon were husky six-footers, powerful, lanky. Cato, a similar build. Owens typed with Hubbard, although more powerful leg muscles. Peacock, like Gourdin, lanky, powerful.

The size of the feet of these men also varied. Owens wears a size six and one-half. I wore an eight, Hubbard an eight. Gourdin, Gordon and Peacock, tens and elevens. So you see these varied from the stocky build to the slender, lanky type, all capable of hurling their bodies through space ahead of their competitors.

Any coach can and will tell you that if he can get the athlete thinking correctly he is hard to beat. And as I have stated before, strange as it may seem, the colored youths have ideals.

Right now in the grade schools are lads with their hearts and minds set on being another Owens or Peacock. And from that burning determination will come another black champion.

Yours in sports, SOL BUTLER, Former World's Champion Broad-Jumper"

Legend meets legend. At the NCAA track and field championship meet, held in Berkeley, California in June 1935, with cameras flashing, questions flying, and handshaking, Butler walked over to where the trim and fit Jesse Owens was being interviewed and stuck out his hand and said, "This is Sol Butler." The two athletes went into a clinch and there were smiles all around. Owens had just finished first in the 100 yard dash, the 220 yard dash, the 220 low hurdles, and the broad jump.

BROAD JUMP STARS

JESSE OWENS   SOL BUTLER
Owens won the 100-meters and the 200-meters in Berlin in 1936 and annexed the Olympic broad jump title. Sol Butler, member of the 1924 Olympic team was not so fortunate. Sol fell during the trials and injured his leg at Antwerp, Belgium. Butler was once national collegiate and national A.A.U. broad jump champion. —Adair Studio, Los Angeles

Photo courtesy of The *Chicago Defender*

Pushing 40 years of age, Butler would still be playing football. He coached and played for the Black Olympics, an all-black team that would travel the West Coast. On Thanksgiving Day in 1935, his team would face an all-white team, the Atlantic Seals at the Atlantic Boulevard Stadium in Los Angeles, California. Both teams were comprised of former college players.

BLACK OLYMPICS

Negro Pro Football Team Under Guidance of Sol Butler, Famed Athlete of Race, to Play Seals

PROFESSIONAL
FOOTBALL
Atlantic Blvd. Stadium
Sunday, Nov. 17, 2:15 p.m.—4h
ATLANTIC SEALS vs.
BLACK OLYMPICS if above

Butler's Colored All-Stars would lose 7-0 before a very enthusiastic crowd and he only played one quarter.

A reporter asked Butler in March 1936 what it took to make long jumps look so easy. "The hardest thing in broad jumping for me," he said, "was learning to relax enough in the last stride to get a good knee bend, and consequently attain the lift I needed. A boy must learn this. He can learn it first by going back a few strides and practicing short runs in order to get this lift. If he does this, the lift and relaxation will become easier when running at full speed."

In 1936, the movie "Showboat" debuted and starred Paul Robeson and Wichita native Hattie McDaniel, and Sol Butler in an uncredited part. He can be seen and heard in the chorus of the song, 'Old Man River', using his magnificent second tenor voice.

Movie still from the 1936 film, "Showboat," starring Paul Robeson. Butler sang in the chorus with his magnificent singing voice. Source—Universal Studios

Manager Suey Welch hired Butler to train his new prize fighter, Charley "Killer" Coates   Source- *Los Angeles Times*

The new year of 1936 saw Butler take to a different kind of sport, training boxers.

Beginning in January with Charley "Killer" Coates in Los Angeles, California and for the next four years, Butler trained such fighters as Dynamite Jackson, Billy White, Joe Law, Orlando Trotter, and Altus Allen. He would train and condition these fighters to get them into prime physical shape. George Halas, owner of the Chicago Bears, was Butler's partner in owning the contract of Allen.

Altus Allen   **Dynamite Jackson**   **Butler with Billy White**

During a visit to Wichita, Kansas in July 1936, he was asked by reporters why so many track records were being broken recently. Butler attributed more specialization in events, along with better equipment and running conditions. "Now when I was running," Butler said, "we had to do a lot of things and do 'em all in one day. We had heats in the 100 meters, the 200 meters, the broad jump, and then we probably had to run a relay. These days, they stretch the track meets out to two days. A man runs most of his qualifying heats the first day and he's rested up well for the second. That's why he can break records. He's fresher. We didn't think much about breaking records, we thought about winning."

While managing Dynamite Jackson, the bantam boxer, he was asked about Joe Louis. Butler stated, "Not to worry about Joe Louis. He's got it and will come back. He got just a little overconfident. He probably got to taking orders from his wife. It was a natural letdown, but Louis isn't finished by any means."

Butler and his fighter, Dynamite Jackson, were in St. Louis on August 7, 1936 for a fight and was asked to be a guest columnist for the *St. Louis Argus* sports page.

August 8, 1937 Source-St. Louis *Post-Dispatch*

In 1937, newspapers across the United States did a series on famous American athletes, and this one featured Butler.

Butler's college alma mater, Dubuque, invited him to be the keynote speaker at its football banquet on December 17, 1937, and he presented the "D" sweaters to the seniors. He spoke on the "Spirit of Old Dubuque" and was met by many of his former teammates, including Johnny Armstrong. While in Dubuque, Butler was interviewed by Ken Murphy, sports editor of the *Dubuque Telegraph-Herald*, and was asked the usual questions. "Well, you know," Butler said, "I played a couple of games this year. The fellows said I was too old and I said 'Wait a minute; I'll tell you what I'll do—I'll just give you a buck for every yard I lose, if you'll give me four bits for every yard I make.' Well sir, I put on a pair of those silk pants—we never had anything like that in my days up on the hill—and I said, 'Who couldn't run in those things?' When questioned about today's football athletes, Butler replied, "You don't see players in the big schools playing for more than 30 minutes out of a game. Why, if they gave us this open stuff they've got now, and the equipment, and the training, and all that stuff, boy, would we have gone to town." While Butler sustained numerous ups and downs in his life to this point, he stated,

"You know, I always figured I should have been a millionaire. Once we were getting ready to have us a half million, when the banks started closed on us. I'm just starting again now."

Butler attending a football game in Dubuque in 1937.   From the University of Dubuque, Charles C. Myers Library Archive

On May 10, 1940, Butler was invited to receive an award for his achievements at the 75 Years of Negro Progress Exposition at the Convention Hall in Detroit, Michigan. Joe Louis was the keynote speaker, and had many of his awards, photos, and boxing gloves on display. Other notable honorees were Eddie Tolum, Willis Ward, Jesse Owens, Fritz Pollard, Paul Robeson, Brud Holland, and Henry Armstrong. The late Rube Foster was also honored as the founder of the first Negro baseball league in 1919.

Butler experienced a very dark day on November 18, 1940, when he found out his brother Benjamin, had died of a heart ailment. The brothers were very close throughout life, with Benjamin being Sol's biggest fan.

SOL BUTLER'S BROTHER DIES

TULSA. Nov. 28—Benjamin F. Butler, 49, brother of famed athlete Sol Butler and a well known athlete in his own right, died here last week of a heart ailment.

Butler's WWII draft registration card from 1942   Source-Steve Miller

A longtime competitor and good friend of Butler's, Charlie Paddock, winner of three Olympics medals, passed on July 21, 1943 in an aviation accident. Butler was devastated. They had run against each other many times over the years, yet when not competing, they visited each other's homes when they lived in southern California.

Butler had a variety of careers after his professional sports career ended. He worked as a recreational director for the Chicago Park and Recreation Department, helping boys in the Washington Park area develop their athletic skills. In September 1946, fifteen young boys were selected to represent the Washington Park team to play five other park teams to eventually establish a city football championship. An impressive ceremony was held at Columbus Park where the teams received their uniforms and met their coaches. The Washington Park team had a stellar lineup for coaching the youngsters, Duke Slater, Henry Springs, Robert Long, and Sol Butler. The team's first public appearance was at the halftime of the Chicago Cardinals-Chicago Bears game at Comiskey Park on October 6. He also worked as a part-time Cook County probation officer, helping those who made bad choices stay on the right track. Butler worked as a talent agent and record producer for Paul Robeson and also served as the assistant director of the Negro Theater Guild and helped book acts for the USO.

Butler left Chicago on May 16, 1952 to visit his sick mother at the Wesley Hospital in Wichita, Kansas. His dear mother, Mary Elizabeth Wellings Butler, passed away on May 25, 1952 and was buried in Maple Grove Cemetery in Wichita, Kansas. He was at her side.

Sol (second row, second from left) was a sports editor for the *Chicago Bee*, a black-owned newspaper.

Butler's residence, as it appears today, at 4903-South Parkway (now MLK Parkway) in Chicago.

He lived on the third floor.

Butler's information as it appeared in the 1950 Cook County census.

Former Dubuque head coach John Chalmers, later a judge in the Chicago area, was interviewed in January 1954 about his star player, Sol Butler. "He was my standby all the time I was there," the judge said. "Sol and the other two boys whose eligibility had been questioned remained to graduate. Sol knew a lot about football. On defense he was our safety man. Before each game I would call him in, diagram the formations of the other team, and instruct Sol on how to direct the line to meet that attack. I told the others, 'Old Sol is playing back and is in good position to see the formations and to see how you men on the line are positioned. When he tells you to move in or out—you've got to do it.' He was smart and a good student. He was particularly good returning punts and most effective hitting off tackle or running the ends. He was fast, shifty, and had the ability to change speeds. He could have played on any Big 10 team."

The last known photograph of Sol Butler was taken in May 1952 in Chicago, Illinois.

During one of Butler's last interviews, he was asked about 'modern' football and he commented that "the boys are pampered too much. Take us. We had to run a mile to the practice field every evening, and we ran back, no buses to haul us out. And we played football all the time, there wasn't a man jumping up every five minutes to take your place. And they tackled hard and they knocked you down from behind. It was mighty rough going. I believe the boys today ride too much to get really tough. They couldn't take it like we did."

On November 30, 1954, it was a cold, bleak night with the temperatures hovering in the low 20's. Butler was working his shift at Pappy's Liquors, at 47th and Cottage Grove on Chicago's south side, as a bartender and bouncer. A patron named Jimmy Hill, entered the bar and began hassling a couple of female customers. Butler swiftly came to their assistance and showed Hill the door. An hour later, Hill returned, armed and intoxicated. He kicked open the door, and began firing at Butler, hitting him several times in the shoulder and the chest. Butler returned fire, wounding Hill with a revolver that was hidden under the bar. Both were rushed to Provident Hospital for treatment, but Butler would take his last breath the following morning, passing from this world on December 1, 1954. Hill would die from his injuries on December11.

Pappy's Liquors where Butler was killed. Source- Preservation Chicago

Butler's funeral was held at the Metropolitan Funeral Parlor in Chicago. When his sister went to his apartment to collect his belongings, it was discovered all his trophies, awards, and athletic accolades were gone. His body was transported by train, accompanied by his sisters Mrs. Anna Gardner and Miss Josephine Butler, and was buried on January 5, 1955 in the Maple Grove Cemetery at 1000-North Hillside in Wichita, Kansas.

Sol Butler's obituary would be listed in newspapers across the country. Once the nation's greatest high school athlete, the second black quarterback in the NFL, holder of world records in several track events and an Olympian, his untimely and unnecessary death shook the country.

SHOT IN LIQUOR STORE BATTLE, BARTENDER DIES

Sol W. Butler, 58, of 4903 South Park way, died yesterday in Provident hospital of bullet wounds suffered Tuesday in a gun battle in Pappy's liquor store, 4700 Cottage Grove av., where Butler was employed as bartender.

Butler was shot by James Hill, 51, of 4720 St. Lawrence, who, in turn, was shot and wounded by the store manager, Harry Wolf, 48, of 2100 Lincoln Park West. Hill is in the Bridewell hospital with bullet wounds in the chest, side, abdomen, and left arm.

Butler many years ago was a member of the American Olympic team in the broad jump event.

Chicago Tribune

Wounds Are Fatal To Solomon Butler

CHICAGO, ILL. (P)—Solomon Butler, 58, one-time athletic star at the University of Dubuque (Iowa), died Wednesday night of bullet wounds suffered in a south side tavern fracas. Butler was a football and track standout at Dubuque in 1920.

Des Moines Register

BUTLER—Solomon, age 58, a veteran of World War I, who died in a Chicago Illinois hospital Wednesday. Funeral services will be 2 p.m. Thursday, November 8 at the St. Paul A.M.E. Church Reverend H. H. Brookins will officiate. Burial will be in the Maple Grove cemetery with the Citizens Funeral Home in charge.

Wichita Eagle

Provident Hospital in Chicago where Butler died from his wounds.

Ex-Rock Island Athlete Shot, Dies At Chicago

Daily Times Davenport, Iowa

Butler, Star Athlete, Is Gun Victim

Rock Island Argus Rock Island, Illinois

After Butler's death, sports writers and athletes across the country recalled their memories about him. George Bretnall, of Iowa State University and the only other Iowan on the Olympic team, had this to say about Butler. "Sol was chosen as the No. 1 jumper. This he did at around 23 feet, as I remember it. His feet and legs sank deep into the soft sand and as he snapped over he pulled a muscle in his thigh. That was it for him. Although he tried again, he was unable to jump effectively," Bretnall continued, "He was bitterly disappointed because his ability rated him first place. He blamed himself for not jumping all out on his first try, but you can't second guess a pulled muscle."

John Shuler of Des Moines, a contemporary of Butler who competed against him while at Davenport High, agrees, "Sol was the greatest natural athlete I saw in my day and I have seen some good ones."

The day after Butler was killed, Davenport *Daily Times* sports editor, John O'Donnell, wrote this in his column about Sol.

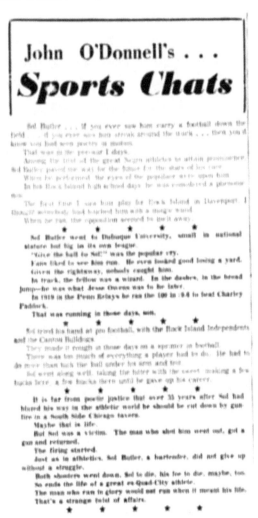

In an extremely moving tribute to Butler, Mrs. J. R. Younquist, the daughter of his college football coach, wrote this about him.

Dear Editor: " *I have just learned of the untimely death of my friend and my father's (Judge J. G. Chambers of Dubuque, Iowa) friend, Solomon Butler. "Sol" was one of Dad's star athetes there many years ago.*

I remember, when I was ten years old, the occasion when my father and mother invited the whole football team over for dinner. I remember how good "Sol" was. I used to sit on his lap and watch him eat watermelon. (Boy how he loved it.) Color made no difference to us and never will. It should never make any difference. God made us all equal.

Thirty years ago, my husband and I visited "Sol" at Washington Park when he was recreation director and also the "Ye Old Time Club" and his apartment on South Parkway. I have talked with him by telephone several times since then. He was a wonderful man and a Christian. No matter if he worked in a tavern. He was earning an honest living.

I know Dad is grieving as I am in Sol's passing. If anybody would be welcome at Gabriels' gates, Sol will be, believe me. God rest his soul. " Source- The *Chicago Defender*

In a column in the *Chicago Defender*, columnist Fay Young had this to say about Sol Butler.

"Solomon W. Butler died Wednesday, December 1, as the shades of night fell over Chicago. And as the day ended so did Butler's life. To those who knew him intimately, he was either just plain "Sol" yet many is the day his friends have heard him refer to himself as "Old Sol" which was his pet expression back in his heyday as a great American athlete.

Butler was shot by one Jimmy Hill early Tuesday morning, November 30, following Hill being ejected from a tavern when Sol worked as a bartender and bouncer.

Hill went home, got a .45 automatic and returned to blaze away at Butler who had objected to Hill, said by the police to have been intoxicated, annoying a waitress. Butler was shot several times in the chest and the abdomen.

Few who daily came in contact with Butler knew him as a former American broad jump champion and a sprinter of national note. Because Sol never talked much about himself. Although 59 years old, he seemed to let bygones be bygones—and seemingly preferred to forget the days of glory. There are those of us who not only liked him, enjoyed his company and laughed with him but remembered when he was prancing up and down the field during championship track and field meets waiting his turn at the broad jump pit. There are fond memories of him as a backfield star for the Canton Bulldogs when they played on Chicago's northside. When the team needed the extra yardage Butler would call the signals "Give it to Ol' Sol" and he could really plough through the line or skirt ends.

We remember him better as a star all-around athlete at Hutchinson, Kansas high school then moving to Rock Island, Illinois, when his coach changed jobs. Sol was a one-man track team. He first attracted attention around here when he came up to Northwestern University at the time the Evanston school held interscholastic track and field championships. Butler won the 100, 200, low hurdles, 440 and running broad jump all in a good day's work. He would come back to repeat the performance at the University of Chicago interscholastic meet.

Other coaches yelled "bloody murder." The national interscholastic body ruled against a boy competing in more than three events. Then finally Northwestern and Chicago U. discontinued the high school meets. Butler was some football player at Rock Island. There was whisperings that he might attend the University of Illinois but he chose the Dubuque, Iowa, college.

Butler was among the nation's top springers, a good collegiate hurdler, and an ace broad jumper. From 1912 to 1923 he ruled the roost as broad jumper. He was National AAU running broad jump champion for several of those years and he won watches, medals and whatnot. His brother, now dead, used to keep a scrapbook full of clippings. Sol's performances at the Drake relays, the Penn relays and other big meets drew the attention of the daily paper sport writers. However, the honors bounced off "Ol' Sol's" back like water off a duck.

Although he played some baseball, not anything to amount to much, and took his fling at tennis where he was daily seen on Mother Seams' court at 31st and Rhodes, his love for basketball is greatly remembered. In fact, he came along about 28 years too soon. He would have been great as a Harlem Globetrotter.

Butler joined the late Virgil Blueitt, Bobby Anderson, Creed Hubbard and others on the Wabash Avenue YMCA Big Five and whipped practically all of the amateur quintets in the middle west and east. Then Sol and Phil Jones, then business manager of the Chicago Defender, decided to form the "Defender Big Five." Ed

Ritchie, Wufang Ward and others got into the picture. The team went east and whipped such clubs as the Loendi Club of Pittsburgh, with the late Cum Posey and "Pimp" Young of Lincoln U. in the lineup; the Carleton Avenue Y team of Brooklyn, the St. Christopher quintet which was made up of members belonging to New York's St. Phillips P.E. Church' Bill Madden's Incorporators and the Smart Set. One of Sol's best friends in the east was the late Romeo Dougherty then of the New York News, owned by George Harris, and later with the Amsterdam News.

We could go on writing and writing about Butler. Space doesn't permit it. Sol worked for the Chicago Defender shortly after he returned to the United States after participation in the Inter-Allied games in Paris in 1919. He was a reporter-or at least was hired to be one but the late Lucius Harper and this writer wondered how Sol ever 'graduated' from the college. We joshed him time and again about it but Ol' Sol just wouldn't lose his temper. He had a flair for writing poetry but got nowhere with that. He took life as it came and went and made the best of it.

Others, who had won fame in athletics, moved ahead. He didn't for some reason which he never discussed. He tried writing a column for the Chicago Bee. He bobbed up as an energetic worker with the Old Tymers Athletic Club. Following the disbanding of the Defender Big Five, Butler played with the Chicago Forty club, one of the Greek letter frat fives, the Savoy Big Five and other teams. His last so-called "big" move in the sport world was when he blossomed out as a manager of Altus Allen, a former Golden Gloves heavyweight champion, whom Butler was positive would be another Joe Louis.

And so the curtain comes down on another act in life's drama and removes from our midst a friendly soul. Maybe fate wasn't as kind to Ol' Sol as it might have been but who are we to question? We take Butler's own philosophy "What has to be will be" It was ever thus.

Source-The Chicago Defender

Butler's headstone in Wichita, Kansas

Son. Brother. Student. Athlete. Veteran. Friend. Author. Husband. Actor. Innovator. Entrepreneur. Coach. Humanitarian. And always with that big smile of his.

Live your dreams.

Nothing great is easily won.

Nothing.

Interesting Sol Butler facts----

--Sol still holds the long jump record at his alma mater, now the University of Dubuque, with a leap of 24 feet, 9 ¾ inches, set back in 1919.

--After Sol's athletic career was over, many other athletes tried to capitalize on his name recognition, even white athletes.

--Rumors abounded that when the Harlem Globetrotters were formed in Chicago in 1926, the coach was going to use Sol's name.

--By the time Sol retired from track and field, he had won 186 medals, 25 championship cups, eight gold shields, and four gold watches.

--Sol was given many nicknames by sports writers such as Black Knight, Dark Ghost, Black Comet, Black Apollo, Smoke, Black Tornado, and The Kansas Whirlwind.

--Many newspaper articles and publications document Butler as participating in the 1924 and 1928 Olympics. This is false, as he lost his amateur status when he began playing football in the NFL.

--Due to Rock Island High School's alternating schedule with Clinton, Iowa High School, Butler missed playing against Duke Slater by one year, but they would become teammates on the Rock Island Independents and adversaries when Sol moved to different teams. They would become lifelong friends.

--Despite his fame as a high school athlete, only four actual photos of Butler exist today from his senior year at Rock Island; two at the University of Chicago and two in possession of this author.

--Butler was ranked as the premier high school athlete in the United States in 1914.

--Butler still holds the record for most touchdowns in one game at Hutchinson (7) and at Rock Island (8).

--Rumors circulated that Sol's brother, Ben, stole his trophies and sold them.

--Coach Herbert Roe had three former athletes in the 1920 Olympics: Sol Butler, M.M. Kirksey, and Dan Scott.

--Due to Butler's dominance in Illinois high school track, the Illinois State Interscholastic body ruled that no prep athlete could compete in only two events and a relay.

--Former Augustana College vice president and treasurer, Dr. Knut Erickson, once played against Butler in a football game in his younger days and stated, "He hit me so hard he about put me out of business."

--Butler is the only RIHS graduate to have played on four football state championship teams in high school, three in Kansas and one in Rock Island.

--Frank Edwards, RIHS Class of 1949, recalls that his father watched Butler play football for the Rock Island Independents and commented that "he was the greatest player he had ever seen."

In 1929, upon completion of Rock Island High School's new Public Schools Stadium, a plaque honoring all prior athletes was erected. Sol's name appears on the left side.

Acknowledgements

I would like to thank the following individuals and institutions for their help in completing this book, either through materials or encouragement.

-Doug Frazer, fellow author, friend, RIHS graduate, history professor at Des Moines Area Community College, and all-around good guy that assisted in the editing of this book. His efforts were invaluable and so much appreciated.

-Brian Hallstoos, history professor at University of Dubuque and Sol Butler expert, author, and friend.

-Paul Waggoneer, Hutchison, Kansas columnist

-The gracious staff of the Rock Island County Historical Society and its outstanding collection of *The Rock Island Argus* newspapers. There is nothing like holding 100-year old newspapers in your hands and reading articles as they were printed then.

-Steve Miller, former football coach at Hutchinson High School and author of *Huddle Up Hutch*

-David Johnson, race director of the Penn Relays

-Josh Rowe, founder of the National High School Track and Field Hall of Fame

-Rock Island High School library archives and their great staff, Mary Mendelin and Amy Curtiss

-Rock Island Public Library

-Augustana College's Tredway Library

-Moline Public Library

-Dubuque *Telegraph-Herald* newspaper archives

-Moline *Daily Dispatch* newspaper archives

-Simon Herrera, Rock Island Independents historian

-Kelsey Yang, University of Chicago

-David Burleson, owner of Westview Plantation

-The Reno County Historical Society

-The University of Dubuque Charles C. Myers Library Archives

-Newspapers.com

-The *Chicago Defender* newspaper

-The *St. Louis Argus* newspaper

-Kevin Leonard, Northwestern University Library Archivist

-Laura Ackley-author of *San Francisco's Jewel City: The Panama-Pacific International Exposition of 1915*

-Michelle Lillis, former Rock Island High School Athletic Director

-Jeff Whitaker, Rock Island High School principal

-Administration of the Rock Island-Milan School District #41 for their support

-Mike Emendorfer, current Rock Island High School Athletic Director for the donation of track programs and correspondence related to Butler's senior year

-An anonymous donor who gave me the original football and track programs from 1914-15 and an original scrapbook of all of Sol's newspaper clippings---priceless

-Charles Butler (no relation to Sol)

-And to my wife and daughter and friends for their support while I went on this adventure. I'm glad I made the journey, it was quite a ride and wouldn't trade it for anything.

Post athletic accolades

-In May 2014, the Solomon Butler Character and Courage Award was introduced by Dan Runkle, Athletic Director at University of Dubuque

-The University of Dubuque's first indoor track meet of each season is named the Sol Butler Invitational

-Induction into Rock Island High School's Athletic Hall of Fame in 1968

-Induction into the University of Dubuque Athletic Alumni Hall of Fame in 1989

-Induction into the inaugural class for the National High School Track and Field Hall of Fame in 2018

This extremely prestigious award was given to Solomon Butler posthumously in 2018 by the National High School Track and Field Hall of Fame in New York City. Since Butler didn't have any living relatives to claim it, it was presented to Rock Island High School.

Examples of the numerous headlines touting Sol's sporting achievements, from high school through the Olympics and beyond. His name was in nearly every newspaper across the country for decades.

BUTLER IS WHOLE SHOW IN CHICAGO

ROCK ISLAND HIGH SCHOOL ATHLETE TAKES HONORS AT NORTHWESTERN MEET.

Ties Two World's Records, Breaks Another and Wins Individual and School Trophies.

DAVENPORT WINS BIG EIGHT MEET

Three Points Ahead of Rock Island in Contest in Which Several Records Fall.

BUTLER THE INDIVIDUAL STAR

Overworked, the Colored Athlete Finally Is Unable to Keep the Hot Pace Set.

SOL BUTLER WINS BROAD JUMP AT THE PENN RELAYS

SOL BUTLER WINS RUNNING BROAD

DUBUQUE COLLEGE STAR BEATS WORLD'S BEST AT INTER ALLIED GAMES.

NEGRO TAKES JUMP WITH 7 4. M

SOL BUTLER GOES TO PHILADELPHIA

TO PARTICIPATE IN SPECIAL EVENTS AT PENN RELAY CARNIVAL.

100-YARD DASH AND BROAD JUMP

Will Run Against Star Speed Boys From Michigan, Princeton, Yale and Other Universities.

EXPECT RECORDS TO BE SHATTERED

BLUE AND WHITE ATHLETES TO SEEK HAWKEYE CONFERENCE PLUMS.

PICK SOL BUTLER AS WINNER

Colored Sprinter Looked For to Grab off Individual Honors—Other Fast Men Entered.

(By Press Club)

REMARKABLE SPEED IS SHOWN BY BUTLER

Butler Received Own Kickoff in 1914 Game

SOPHOMORES WIN ON INDOOR TRACK

SCORE THIRTY-SEVEN POINTS AT DUBUQUE GERMAN COLLEGE AND SEMINARY.

INDIVIDUAL HONORS TO BUTLER

Negro Star Lands Three Firsts— Freshmen Crowd the Sophs. Scoring 29 Points.

SOL BUTLER GOES EAST

BUTLER IS ENTERED IN NEW YORK MEET

COLORED STAR IS TO COMPETE WITH FASTEST MEN IN THE WORLD.

MEETS DREW AND MEREDITH

Entered in 60-Yard and 300-Yard Dashes and the 70-Yard High Hurdles.

BUTLER WINS AGAIN IN 100 METER DASH

AMERICAN ATHLETES PROMINENT IN LIST OF VICTORIES IN INTER-ALLIED GAMES.

BUTLER'S BUNCH ARRIVES FOR GAMES

Sol Butler of Dubuque Wins Leading Event of America's Greatest Track Meet

Butler is hailed as the greatest high school athlete in the United States at the present time.

WEDNESDAY—THE ROCK ISLAND ARGUS—OCTOBER 8, 1924

Sol Butler Coming With Hammond Team

SOL BUTLER STARS; WINS FIVE EVENTS

DUBUQUE NEGRO TIES SHORT
DASH MARK AND BREAKS
JUMP FIGURES.

COE WINS MEET; DUBUQUE SECOND

SOL TO TRY FOR AMERICAN TEAM

Butler Will Compete Against Central
West Stars at Stagg's Field
Saturday.

TO ENTER TRIALS UNATTACHED

Loomis, Simpson, Smith, Marks and
Other Celebrities to Run Against
Colored Star.

BUTLER SCORES 26 POINTS AND LANDS INDIVIDUAL HONORS

SHEER WEIGHT IS RESPONSIBLE FOR ISLANDERS' LOSS

Rock Island High School Fails
to Stop Fierce Attack of
Davenport Backs.

BUTLER INDIVIDUAL STAR

Sol Sprints 95 Yards for Score in First
Game in Seven Years for Tri-
City Championship.

SOL BUTLER WINS INDIVIDUAL HONOR

LOCAL COLORED STAR TAKES
FIRST IN THREE EVENTS, DE-
FEATING LOOMIS.

ALEDO WALLOPED BY R. I. 76 TO 0

Local High School Walks Away With First Regular Game in Easy Fashion.

DISPLAYS SCORING ABILITY

Ackley, Gleason, Whisler and Butler Play Stellar Game—Visitors Wilt Under Attack.

SOL BUTLER TO TRY TO BREAK WORLD RECORD

Former Rock Island High Athlete Entered in Central A. A. U. Games at Chicago.

BUTLER WILL TRY AGAIN

ENTERS CENTRAL A. A. U. INDOOR MEET AT EVANSTON NEXT SATURDAY.

SEND RELAY TEAM TO PENNSYLVANIA

DUBUQUE GERMAN COLLEGE AND SEMINARY AFTER HONORS AT PHILADELPHIA.

BUTLER TO MEET SPEEDY BOYS

Colored Streak Entered in 100-Yard Dash and Broad Jump—Will Go Against Smith.

RAISING FUND TO AID SOL BUTLER

Rock Island High School Alumni Take Lead in Subscription to Pay Prince Expense.

GOOD ADVERTISEMENT FOR CITY

Want to See That Rock Island Colored Man Is Not Handicapped by Lack of Cash.

BUTLER SENSATION OF DRAKE CARNIVAL

DUBUQUE STAR PUTS SPECTACULAR FINISH TO ½-MILE RELAY AND PLACES IN DASH.

SOL BUTLER IS GIVEN PLACE IN ALLIED GAMES

COLLEGE ATHLETES FEASTED AT JULIEN

"GREATER ATHLETICS" IS KEYNOTE OF BANQUET TENDERED MEMBERS "D" CLUB.

BUTLER DELIVERS FAREWELL TALK

Famous Colored Star Finishes Collegiate Course—Has Won Fame for College.

BUTLER EQUALS WORLD RECORD FOR 60 YARDS

Feat of Rock Island Negro Features Games Held at Northwestern.

ISLANDERS HOLD PANHANDLERS TO 0 TO 0 VERDICT

Cleveland Gains Most Ground but Lacks Punch to Cross Line.

BAHAN'S DROPKICK FAILS

Butler, Islander Flash, Marked Man; Great Crowd Views Combat.

SOL BUTLER WINS RUNNING BROAD

DUBUQUE COLLEGE STAR BEATS WORLD'S BEST AT INTER ALLIED GAMES.

NEGRO TAKES JUMP WITH 7 4. M

BROAD JUMPER PULLS TENDON

SOL BUTLER GETS DESERVED FAVORS

Star Colored High School Athlete Invited to Attend Pan-American Exposition.

WILL ALSO GO TO CHICAGO

Entered in the 50 Yard Dash, Hurdles and the Broad Jump—First Basketball Practice.

JOIE RAY SETS NEW 500-METER RECORD

COVERS DISTANCE IN 1 MINUTE, 7 SECONDS AS AMERICANS BEGIN TRAINING.

BUTLER TAKES TURNS AT JUMP

Dubuque Athlete Among Those Who Began Limbering Up at Antwerp Monday.

GREAT SPRINTERS TO DRAKE RELAY

FASTEST MEN IN WEST TO COMPETE IN ANNUAL SPRING CLASSIC.

BUTLER OF DUBUQUE AMONG STARS

Blue and White Sends Half-Mile Relay Team and Star Enters 100-Yard Dash.

BUTLER'S ABSENCE AROUSES COMMENT

FAILURE OF DUBUQUE STAR TO COMPETE IN STATE MEET DISAPPOINTS FANS.

READY FOR THE PARISIAN GAMES

Expect Word From A. A. U. Soon In Regard to Inter-Allied Meet.

PICK CHICAGO TO WIN 'BIG 9' MEET

MAROONS EXPECTED TO SCORE FIRST IN ALL THE FIELD EVENTS.

PICK BUTLER IN BROAD JUMP

Dubuque College and Seminary Star Says He Will Win the 220-Yard Dash.

TO GO AFTER WORLD TITLE

Sol Butler, in Fine Shape, to Try for Sprint Championship.

FOOTBALL AT DUBUQUE

Has Been Chosen Captain of Track Team For 1917—Retirement of Drew a Big Help.

BUTLER SETS NEW JUMPING RECORD

Colored Marvel Leaps 25 Feet 2½ Inches in Tryouts at Stagg's Field Saturday.

BUTLER PLACED ON STATE TEAM

Star Colored Back of Rock Island High Assigned Position of Full Back.

WILLIS IS GIVEN A PLACE

Sol is Rated as Greatest Prep Player in State of Illinois—Was Sensation of the Season.

Joe Louis And Other Great Negro Athletes Will Be Presented Trophies At Exposition

YANKEE BREAKS OLYMPIC MARK; BUTLER IS OUT

Landon, N.Y.A.C., Sets New High Jump Record—"Sol" Injured, Fails to Qualify.

ISLANDERS TRIM OTTAWA 53 TO 0

Local High School Eleven Adds Another Win to List of Victories.

LOOBY AND GAETJER STAR

Butler Shows Well at Quarterback and Hinkley Shines in Backfield—Scrubs Beat Moline.

BUTLER TO BE PILOT
WHILE FLATTERY AND
SPECK TAKE GUARDS

Sol Butler Is Latest Star To Join Strong Bulldog Roster

'Sol' Butler, Famed Athlete, Slain

The last headline Butler would get, the day after he was killed.

The following book was written by Solomon and his brother Ben, while seniors at Rock Island High School, in the hope that the profits would fund Sol's education at Harvard. Those dreams never materialized, although he did sell several hundred copies of it. Please enjoy *"Three Years of High School Athletics."*

Three Years

Of

High School Athletics

A narrative of athletic experiences on the

Grid iron and track

By

Sol and Ben Butler

"Labor conquers all things"

Purpose

We hope someday to take our stand as leaders of our race.

To do this we must have a liberal education. We have written this book as a means to this end.

PREFACE

By Coach Herbert N. Roe

Director of Athletics, Rock Island High School, formerly coach and instructor in English, Hutchinson, Kansas

I wish to recommend this little volume to anyone interested in athletics and to all who believe that sincerity of purpose, ambition, and real ability should be recognized, wherever found. I have known the writers for several years and have found them in every way deserving of success and recognition. Sol Butler is now recognized as the champion high school athlete in the country; and has great promise of holding the world's title. He was won his place through hard work, sacrifice and determination. He is the most reliable and conscientious of all the athletes I have worked with, and in addition to being a wonderful performer, has exceptional qualities that stand for character and manhood.

Chapter One

I was born in Oklahoma, seven miles from the present site of Kingfisher, March 3, 1895. My father was a slave, but my mother a free born woman. Our family, which is composed of two boys and two girls, endured many hardships that naturally follow the opening of a new country. By a piece of misfortune, my father lost his farm and we moved to Kingfisher to live. We stayed there about ten years, after which my people moved to Wichita, Kansas. I was then in the third grade. Four years later, we moved to Hutchinson, Kansas, where my parents live now. I shall always remember Hutchinson as a city where people really do things, because it is there that the older people encourage the children and young people in every form of outdoor sport. I was in the seventh grade when I went to Hutchinson and I immediately became interested in playing grade football. I gained a very good idea of the game and determined to play and made a very good success as a grade player, and when I entered high school, in 1912, everyone predicted that I would make good.

I was exceedingly anxious to succeed, because it is not every freshman who has the honor or chance to rub shoulders with the jolly juniors or the grave seniors. The first evening I donned a pair of football pants I felt that life could not hold any greater boon than the wearing of this respected armor. But the worst was yet to follow, in the form of scrimmages and learning to tackle. After about two hours of hard work I began to realize the truth of the saying,"that nothing great is lightly won." We kept this practice up every afternoon for about two weeks. When the coach had practically decided on the men whom he thought fit to represent the school on the gridiron, he admonished us to train hard. On account of my being a colored boy a few of the boys objected to my playing on the team, but after they had learned to know me better, and found I at all times was guided by the same principles of good behavior and gentlemanly conduct as themselves, they welcomed me as one of them. I can truthfully say that there never was a "whiter" bunch of boys than those who represented the gold and blue during the time I took part in athletics as a representative of Hutchinson high school.

The first game of the season of 1913 was played with Stafford high school, but I was unable to take part in this game because the visitors objected to playing against colored boys. I did not feel the least bit discouraged, because I realized that there are certain conditions that every man and every race has to overcome, and I was determined to prove to all Kansas that there was not a player in the state who had received any better home training than myself, or any better ideas of what constituted true sportsmanship and fair play. However, when we went to Lyons, Kansas and this team also refused to play against colored players, after having used one themselves. Coach Yeoman and Captain McCandless pulled out team off the field and refused to play without his two colored players. Lyons finally reconsidered her objection, and Phillips, another colored lad, and myself, were allowed to take part in the game. From that time on we never had any more trouble that year, because the coach, who was one of the smartest men I have ever had the pleasure of working with, championed our cause when the argument of this nature arose.

By having the best percentage of any football team in the state, and by going through the season undefeated, we were the recognized state champions. The success of this team was due largely to the efficient coaching of Don O. Yeoman, our athletic instructor, who made of the team one of the fastest and smoothest running machines in the state. However, the hard, conscientious training of the players made possible that which coaching could not have accomplished, and the loyal students of the school contributed their share in the way of support. There were six all-state men on the team—Captain McCandless, right half; Hiram Patten, fullback; Fay Prickett, right end; Joe Gleadall, right tackle; George Duckworth, quarterback; and myself; left halfback.

After the passing of a very successful football season, our school was still creditably represented by a worthy five in basketball, but I did not care to play the game, as it did not then appeal to me. I thought that I could be of greater service to the school as a track man. I had never taken part in any track events before this time, but a number of critics who had seen my work on the football field thought I could make good. With this encouragement I started out at the opening of the season to do my best to make the team and help "put Hutchinson on the map." The members of the track team were: Ralph Pattinson, Ernest Friesen, Bobby Bacon, Clarence Phillips, Darwin Pattinson, Russell Armstrong, William Hughes, Minot English, and myself. Our first meet was a dual meet with Stafford, which we won by a large score. This so encouraged us that we continued to train in order to keep up our winning streak. Yeoman was a man who could inspire you to do your utmost by speaking to you before a game or a meet. He was a forceful talker, and after he had told us of our defects, he proceeded to help us to remedy them. We worked hard after the Stafford meet to be in readiness for the Seventh District meet, held at Sterling on the following Saturday. The day of this meet we were in fine condition and we entered the meet determined to give our opponents a real exciting time. There were about six schools represented, with 100 athletes, and we won easily. I was fortunate enough to win the following events: 100-yard dash in 10 2/5 seconds, the 220 in 26 seconds, the 220 hurdles in 29 and the broad jump by a leap of over 19 feet. By making the highest number of points of any athlete on the field, I was awarded a solid gold medal. The school also received a beautiful cup in recognition of the ability of the athletes. The winning of this meet caused great rejoicing in the camp of Hutchinson high school and it made us feel as if we could accomplish anything when so loyally supported by the student body and faculty. By this time the track squad of the high school was recognized as a startling reality, instead of a mere possibility. We were still eager to try our skill against the best teams that our neighboring schools could produce.

At this time Great Bend had a colored lad by the name of Porter, who was reputed to be the fastest man in western Kansas and one of the fastest in the state. He and I had never met except on the football field, and the people of our respective towns were in doubt as to the superiority of one over the other. The people of Hutchinson thought that I was capable of beating Porter, but his townspeople thought that he was more experienced than I, was better developed, and in fact was the faster man. He had established a good reputation as a sprinter and had gained the confidence of his friends and schoolmates. It was the Saturday after the meet at Sterling that Porter and I toed the line together in the Central Kansas meet in my hometown. The excitement was intense. The supporters of both of us were giving their opinions as to the number of feet that would separate us at the finish.

In all of my races, and during the whole of my athletic career, I have never allowed myself to become excited. I take things in a matter of fact way and I never believe that my opponent is a better man until he has proven it to me. In other words, I take nothing for granted; I care not for past achievements, I do not respect the significance of name, but I do respect real ability.

There were about 35 of us in the 100-yard dash and we ran it off in heats, the first and second men qualifying for the finals. As luck would have it, Porter and I had to run our preliminary heat together. He was a fine specimen of an athlete and as he limbered up, I could see that he had the proper leg muscles to run any kind of a race. But when the starter cried, "Get to your marks," I noticed that he seemed to be nervous and to go into the race in a half-hearted way. There were three other boys in the race besides ourselves, but the main interest lay in how we were going to finish. In a few moments after we had prepared for starting the starter cried, "On your marks." I kneeled down to the first position. "Get set!" I called all my wits into play and looked down the alley in which I was to run until I had located the tape. "Crack!" went the pistol and we were off, running for school and honor. For the first fifty yards we ran neck and neck, then I called all of my strength into play and darted ahead, so that at the finish I had beat Porter by about five feet. His schoolmates were dumbfounded and refused to believe that he had run his best. They comforted themselves in the belief that their man was reserving his strength and would surely beat me in the final race. I have since learned by experience that if you can beat your man in the preliminary, you can do it, with a few exceptions, in the final. I managed to beat all my opponents in the final heat in 10 2/5 seconds, took first place in the broad jump, making more than 19 feet, won the 220 hurdles and took second in the 220 dash. The track being muddy—rain having set in after the finish of the 100-yard dash—the time of the last races was very slow. Still, we were glad that we had won this meet against such keen competition. The rest of the men on the team also won points, and we won by double the score of our next closest opponent.

Our next meet was at Lawrence, Kansas, and Coach Yeoman was anxious to win the meet, or make a good showing. Lawrence being a college town, all of its athletes are very enthusiastic over an athletic contest of any kind. This was a state meet, and we knew that some of the best athletes in the state would be there. Lawrence had won the interscholastic meet ever since its origin, and we realize that it would be a great honor to our school and city if we could make a creditable showing. Our ambition did not soar to such heights that we had visions of winning this meet, because we realized that four men against two well-trained track teams entered by Lawrence, were going to have all that they could do to even place in their events. All the visiting athletes were struggling against two Lawrence combinations, quality and quantity. Their coach had established a reputation for winning either by real ability or superior generalship. We arrived at Lawrence the evening before the meet and were well entertained by representatives of the school. The next day we spent the forenoon visiting the various departments of the university. However, my mind was busy over the coming events. The coach had entered us in this manner- Butler, 100 and 220-yard dashes; broad jump and 220 hurdles; Freisen, 440 yard dash; Darwin Pattinson, pole vault and Ralph Pattinson, high jump.

The meet was to be called at 1:30 and about 45 minutes before the time the spectators began to arrive. The day was ideal and the sun shone warm and bright. The track was in fine condition, and the three hundred or more athletes on the field, representing the colors of 36 or more schools, made a very impressive spectacle. The different yells from the loyal rooters of these institutions caused the blood to course quicker through the veins of many a stalwart athlete who realized that he was not running for himself alone, but for the honor of his school, the people of his community, and his home. Presently the lively music of the band indicated that the events would soon be started. Then we heard the call of the starter announcing the first event and the class of the various schools taking part. According to their enrollment, the schools were placed in class A, B, or C. There were six schools in the first class, and they were all represented by capable athletes.

We went out on the track to limber up, and as I jogged up and down, I distinctly heard the different comments of the crowd.

"Can he run?" "Where is he from?" "He looks more like a farmer than a runner."

"Just wait until he bobs alongside of little Bill Wright." Bill will make him look like a novice!"

"Last call for the fifty-yard dash!" announced the starter.

There were six of us in the race and it was to be run off in one heat. We drew numbers for the choice of alleys, and I was lucky enough to draw first choice. I took the third, thinking it would give me the best advantage. Wright, the best sprinter from Lawrence High, was next to me in the second alley. I found him a game little fellow, and he had not been beaten by a high school man. All of the college boys were confident that he was able to defeat any man in that part of the country.

"On your marks!" cried Grover, one of the best starters in the west. We went to our alleys, ready for the next order.

"Get set!"

We called our wits and nerves into play.

"Crack!"

We were off like shots. I forged ahead and breasted the tape the winner in 5 3/5 seconds, in one of the fastest races I have ever run. You can imagine the consternation that seized the Lawrence rooters when it became evident that I had really beaten Wright. They found consolation in the thought that the fifty-yard event was not Wright's race and that he would surely 'come back' in the 100. Five points for Hutchinson! I realized that our school was not going to pass unrecognized. I looked over to the place where they were pole vaulting and saw that Pattinson was holding his own. "Little Pat's" closest competitor was Edwards, of Jewell City. Both were making a hard fight for first place. When they reached 10-6 it was nip and tuck, and the interest in the contest had reached fever heat. "Little Pat" said, "eleven feet." The crowd looked at him as if it thought he had suddenly done crazy. Edwards looked around with a confident smile on his face and said, "I don't care how high they put it."

Pat started down the path with the pole well balanced, and with a might leap cleared the bar two or three inches. Edwards made three unsuccessful attempts to clear the bar, and acknowledged himself beaten, and little Pat was proclaimed the winner. Five points more for Hutch! When the height was measured and sag allowed for, it was found that he had broken the state record by four and a half inches.

While I was rejoicing over this victory, I was called to run the 100-yard dash. I was as successful in that as in the 50, making it in 10 1/5 seconds, breaking the state record by a fifth of a second. When the final count was mad ewe found that we had won second place in the meet, taking 27 ½ points to Lawrence's 39. We were happy to know that we had made a name for our school. "Little Pat" and I were both awarded loving cups for breaking records, and I was also given the individual cup in Class A for winning the highest number of points.

On the following Saturday we went to the Arkansas Valley Interscholastic meet at Wichita. On account of a little misunderstanding in regard to a race run between Whetmore, Wichita's crack sprinter, and myself, Coach Yeoman refused to continue in the meet and we withdrew, after I had won the 100 and 220 yard dashes, and two more medals. This meet practically finished our track season for the year 1912, and we were satisfied at the showing we had made. We had added many cups to the high school trophy case and were proud that the school had been recognized as one of the first rank in athletics as well as scholarship. With this feeling we began our vacation, determined to preserve ourselves to the best of our ability in order to do the same good work when school should start in the fall. We lost some good football and track men by graduation.

CHAPTER TWO

When the football season of 1912 opened, we were weakened a great deal by the loss of some of our star players. McCandless, Patten, Prickett and Gleadall were among those absent. Mr. Yeoman started to coach the old and new material into a smooth-running machine. The new men who made the team were Milfred Hartman, Bill Hayes, Chauncey Yeoman and John Foster. We worked hard to get the team up to the proper standard, and then we again entered the camp of the Sterling boys. Bobby Bacon played halfback and George Duckworth quarter. We found the Sterling team much weaker than we had supposed, and instead of a football game it was a track meet, for there was not a player on our team who did not make some kind of a dash across the goal line. The final score was 78-0. We next met Stafford on our home field and played them to a tie. We should have won the game; but played like a bunch of novices. It is my experience in athletics that no matter how well trained a team is, there are times when the majority of the players don't play their usual game. I do not know what accounts for this, but most coaches say it is due to a certain mental strain which spreads over the whole team and makes them "sticks," as far as head work is concerned. In the second game of the season we were defeated by Wichita by a score of 21 to 13. She won the game by fighting hard; and played us off our feet in the second half. Wichita has always been noted for school spirit and fighting spirit, and it was here that I first realized that the two make a combination that is hard to beat. We entered the game over-confident, and when we found that we were up against a bunch of real players we were unable to overcome their courage. We felt very bad on account of this defeat, because it was the first game, we had lost in two seasons. A defeat is sometimes good for a team, since it takes away that feeling of overconfidence, which produces a spirit of indifference to training. If you lose fairly you should have nothing to be ashamed of, and can only give the credit to whom it is due.

During the season of 1912 we defeated Pratt, Nickerson, Salina, Wichita (second game) and Kingman. The hardest game was with the team of Pratt high school. She was represented by one of the best teams in the state, and they averaged in weight about 160 pounds, while our average was 155. On the game of the game the Pratt rooters came to Hutchinson 300 strong. This was considered a large crowd, because it is seldom that the Kansas people will follow a high school team around. The day was ideal for football, being neither too warm, or too cool; and everyone was pleased with the prospect of ideal conditions. This game had been well advertised and the rivalry between the two cities was at fever heat. The general interest in the contest and the ideal weather conditions brought out a crowd of over two thousand. We were supported by a loyal bunch of rooters and the city band turned out in full regalia to do honor to the occasion. The Pratt team had not been defeated up to that time and was considered to be invincible by its students and citizens. A 2 o'clock the park was crowded. The sporting element of both cities were mingling together, laying wagers on the outcome of the game. At 2:30 the referee blew his whistle and the game started amid great cheering by the rooters of both teams. The ball was first in Pratt's territory and then in ours. The backfield men of both teams would make gains of a few yards and then the opposing lines would hold like a stone wall for three straight downs. This was before the four down system was inaugurated. This was kept up until the whistle blew at the close of the first half. Both teams went to their resting places and the rooting among the spectators increased. The coach came over to us and began to talk to us as only a real coach can, telling us our weaknesses and instilled into us that fighting spirit that is a real necessity to a football team.

When the second half started, we determined to do our best to uphold the honor of H.H.S. The first quarter of the second half ended with a score of 0-0. The last quarter began with both teams fighting harder than ever, but after a few downs we got the ball in Pratt's territory on her 45-yard line. Our heady little quarterback, Duckworth, was doing his best to outgeneral his opponent. On the third down we had about five yards to go. He called my signal for an end run. The ball was quickly passed to me and I was off like a flash. I tried to circle the end, but I could see that he was going to get me unless I changed my course. I saw an opening directly through center. I took my chance and darted through the hole. I made about ten yards, but did not stop, for directly in front of me I saw one of the Pratt men ready to tackle me. I changed my course and, by a burst of speed, made ten yards more. I realized that if I could keep this up I could reach the covered goal. I dashed ahead and collided with one of the largest players in a head-one collision. He fell before my onslaught, but I still kept my feet.

Look! Directly in front of me stood the goal posts. It seemed to be only a few feet away, and with one supreme effort I cleared the remaining space. The great cheer that went up from the grand-stand and the congratulations of my teammates made me feel that I could sacrifice anything in return for such loyal support. We missed the goal and the score stood at 6-0. Pratt came back and after a few minutes succeeded in getting a touchdown and kicking goal. We were not discouraged, though it looked as if we had struggled in vain. We had only about three minutes to play. Bacon, our right halfback, succeeded in getting away and carried the ball within five yards of Pratt's goal. Our opponents held us for two downs like a stone wall, and on the third Duckworth called me for an end run. I faked a buck through the line, then circled the end for the final touchdown of the game. We kicked goal and the curtain went down on one of the hardest games that I had ever played, with the score standing 13 to 6 in our favor.

We finished the football season with one defeat chalked up against us. This we made up for by defeating Wichita in a second game, 28-0. At the close of the football season Coach Yeoman resigned his position, and we were all certainly sorry to see him leave. He had worked hard with the team and had given every player a good idea of the principles of football.

The basketball season was hardly over before every ambitious athlete in the school was working out on the track. In a short time, all the available material had been tried out and the coach decided on the following men worthy of the honor of representing the school: Friessen, Ralph Pattinson, Darwin Pattinson, Bill White, Clarence Phillips and myself. The season began with the seventh district meet, held at Pratt. We were up against some of the best men in the state, with 35 schools represented by 200 athletes. We won the school cup for the highest number of points, the championship relay cup, while I won the individual cup for taking the greatest number of points.

Our next meet was at Lawrence, where we met the same class of men from the different schools that we had competed against the previous year. My old opponent, Wright, of Lawrence, had been training during the year for the avowed purpose of beating me, but I breasted the tape ahead of him in every event in which we were entered. I received the surprise of my life in the 50-yard dash, and this is how it happened: Wright, Hardy, of Kansas City, and myself placed in the preliminaries. In the final race I took the middle alley, with Hardy on my right and Wright on my left. I was watching Wright, because I thought him the better of the two. At the crack of the gun we started for the tape. Ten yards from the finish I saw that I had Wright beaten and began to slow up a little. Imagine my surprise, when just as I was about five yards from the finish, I saw Hardy pass me as if I was not running at all. I was so shocked that I felt as if I was in a dream. The crowd was surprised and continued to shout "Hardy beat Butler." I learned a valuable less from that race and I decided that I would never slack up in a race again until I was two yards across the finish. I have since discovered that the finish is far more important than the start. Many an athlete gets off good, but falls down about 15 yards from the tape and fails to "produce the goods."

The only way to "produce the goods" in athletics is to lead a clean, moral life and train earnestly the year around. I attribute my success in athletics to the following out of these two ideas. I have heard people say a number of times, "the reason he is a good athlete is that he has a strong physique." But they are mistaken in their ideas. How many strong men have you seen who could not stand up under a severe strain, who could not pass the endurance test? Endurance is the life of an athlete, and the only way you can have it is to live a life free from the evils that destroy vitality and shipwreck useful lives.

In the meet at Lawrence I defeated Hardy in the 100-yard dash in 10 3/5 seconds. I also won the 220, the 220 hurdles, and was second in the broad jump, giving me 21 points. Our school took second place again and we gave Lawrence a real scare.

We won the A.V.I. meet at Wichita the following Saturday and I again won the 100, 220-yard dashes, 220 hurdles, the broad jump and came in second in the shot-put. The last meet of the season was at Manhattan, Kansas, under the auspices of the State Agricultural College. We won the meet with a large score, also the relay in fast time. "Little Pat" won the pole vault, as usual. I won the individual cup here, and although the Topeka Daily Capitol advertised that they would give a cup to the individual point winner, I have yet the first time to see it. That paper owes me the cup and I hope that I will receive it at some future date, when the promise is remembered. In addition to winning firsts in the 50, 100, and 220-yard dashes, 220 hurdles and shot-put, I broke every previous record in these events made by high school athletes at this school. I also won second in the broad jump and ran in the relay. This closed our season, and I can truthfully say that every man on the team deserved praise for the way he trained for his respective events. Although some were better than others, all showed true school spirit, true grit, and possessed a high standard of morality.

The people of the world are the same in every clime and state in some respects. When they see a man struggling hard to make a success in life, encouragement and sympathy are extended to him. Even if he fails to make as good a showing as a more fortunate individual, they say to themselves, "Well, I am for him because he did his best." After a man has put forth every effort to succeed and then fails, he really deserves as much credit as the one who is more fortunate than himself.

During vacation I always keep in training, as I realize that in order to be successful an athlete must take the best of care of his body at all times. I generally play baseball during the summer months, or take up some form of outdoor sport, consequently when school starts in the fall I am in good condition.

Hutchinson high school was fortunate enough to secure H.N. Roe of Colorado Springs, Colorado, for director of athletics for the year 1913-14. Mr. Roe had a good reputation as coach in Colorado, and we began our work under him with high hopes. We had some good football material to work with and succeeded in turning out a team that won the championship of Kansas. We met the strongest teams in the state and won all our games but one. We finished the season with a great gridiron battle at Salina for the state title and won by a score of 34-12 before a crowd of 3000 people. Several teams who were said to be in the running for championship honors refused to play us on account of there being two colored players on the Hutchinson team. About this time, it seemed that a number of the schools had banded together and adopted resolutions refusing to play against colored boys. Pratt and Wichita were two schools who made such an excuse for not playing us. Hutchinson would send out her challenges and they would be accepted, and then about a week before the game they would tell us that they had "drawn the color line." This did not make me feel badly on my own account, because I have been subjected to numerous difficulties of this nature since birth, but I felt that Hutchinson was not getting a square deal in the matter. The same schools that were making these objections had been represented by colored players. Taking these things into consideration I made up my mind that, as much as I hated to leave, I would have a better chance of continuing my work without such an abundance of objectives and hard feelings. I had always been well treated by the student body and townspeople of Hutchinson, and it was with deep regret that I finally left dear old Hutchinson high school and started out to seek athletic success and my high school diploma elsewhere.

Our football team that fall was the best team I ever played on; and worked as a machine during the whole season. This was the result of good coaching, proper training, and real school spirit. We began to use the open style of play, in shift formations that usually dazed our opponents. Our defense was the most wonderful I have ever seen. Teamwork was our motto, and "every man in every play." We were defeated by Marion early in the season, when several good men were on the hospital list, but came back strong and piled 266 points to our opponents 68. The following are clippings from the High School Buzz in regard to the players:

"The football season of 1913 was one of splendid victories for Hutchinson high school. We met some of the strongest teams in the state and won every game but one. We finished the season with a great gridiron battle at Salina, when we defeated the champions of the northern half of the state, 34-12, before 2500 people. We have a better claim to championship honors than any team in Kansas; Wichita, Lawrence and Pratt refusing to accept our challenge. Coach Roe's men worked as a machine during most of the season, using the open style of play in shift formations. Our defense proved to be invincible for high school teams and we met the heavy charging of the United States soldiers and the dashing track play of the Salina tam with equal success. The men showed proper spirit and mad teamwork their motto."

"Our schedule was a poor one from a financial point of view, and we failed to make a resource fund for track. We did pay $60 left over from the year before, however. The season ticket plan should have been adopted, which would have insured better patronage. Next year we have been promised a Thanksgiving Day game with Salina and we can hope Pratt will not get 'cold feet.'

"Sol Butler, the whirlwind halfback and track man of Kansas, was the sensation of the gridiron this year. His wonderful playing was worth going miles to see. He is quick as a bullet on offense and a sure tackler. He is 'heady' at critical times and never knows what it is to give up.

"Captain English was a main spring of a well-balanced team. He made a good captain, was a hard fighter, and played his position with credit at all times. Yeoman, captain-elect for next year, was one of the most valuable men on the team. He is cool, shifty, a sure tackler, and can gain ground with the ball when called upon. Duckworth, who played his last year at quarter and half, was easily the best man 'at his job' in Kansas. He hit the line like a veteran and never lacked the 'pep' needed to run the team. Phillips, Foster and Smith never failed to out-play their men, and their equals would be hard to find in any high school. Ellsworth, Woodson and Rexroad finished the season playing a strong game. Clinton, Nichols, Wyman and J. Armstrong, all played their positions well. Johnny, at quarter, was the sensation of many of our games. Knieper made his letter by gritty playing. He knows the game; and should play a smashing half next year."

Coach Roe was a great favorite among the boys and girls of all the schools of the city, and all of us wanted to win for him as well as for the school. I have met many men and I have dealt with many, but I have never met one like Coach Roe. He is a man of sterling character, high moral ideas and is very broad minded. He never does any little mean tricks that some coaches do, and, in fact, most of us are subject to doing. I think he would have made a good preacher if he had not been a coach. Yet with all of his other qualities, he stands high as a coach and knows every angle of the athletic game. He is able and willing to help and instruct all those who will listen to him, and I have steadily improved by listening to his coaching. It is due to him that I have acquired many good points that have enable me to make good in big contests and fast meets.

After the football season, the basketball team very creditably represented us in that line of sport. Early in the spring the coach received a letter from Mr. Omer, of Northwestern University, inviting him to send representatives to the indoor meet, March 26-27, at Evanston, Illinois. After a lot of work on the part of Coach Roe and Principal S. L. Palmer, it was planned that I should go, on account of my being considered the best athlete to represent the school. The coach being extremely busy at that time, could not go with ne and I was accompanied by my brother Ben, who is at all times my constant companion. When I left for Chicago very few people thought that I stood any chance to win anything at Northwestern, and I felt that my real chance in athletics was coming.

We arrived in Chicago the day before the meet and proceeded to Evanston, where we met Lewis Omer, athletic director of the university. He showed us over the Patten gym, and I was greatly impressed with the size and wonderfulness of the structure. We were entertained at the home of A. L. Jones, one of the wealthiest and most influential colored citizens of Evanston. I felt the responsibility that rested on me and I knew that my people and friends at home were anxiously waiting to know if I had placed in any of the events, even if I did not win. I felt determined to hold up the prestige of Hutchinson high school, and Coach Roe. I shall long remember the scene in the Patten gym, the night of March 27. There was great excitement and bustle among the athletes from 35 school, but I felt that if ever in my life I was to be cool headed now was the time. The first race that was called was the 60-yard dash. I won my heat in 6 3/5 seconds, which was good as any of my opponents had done in the preliminaries. The winning of this race placed me in good standing with all of the college students, who cheered and encouraged me to do my best. I next placed in the 60-yard high hurdles; my time being 8 1/5 seconds, which equaled the conference record. I next placed in the broad jump, shot-put, and 440, which more or less astonished the crowd and gave me the good will of everyone, and a lot of write-ups in the Chicago papers. The night of the 28th was the real night, for only those who had qualified the night before were eligible to take part.

My first trial in the competition of semi-national athletics was in every way successful. I won the final in the 60-yard dash in 6 2/5 seconds, equaling the world's record. In the 60-yard high hurdles I also equaled the world's record; but was disqualified for knocking down more than two hurdles. I was successful enough to win first in the broad jump with a leap of 20 feet 4 inches. I was beaten in the shot-put and 440. Nevertheless, I was perfectly satisfied with the outcome. I took fourth place for my school and won the individual honors. I found the officials, students and authorities at Northwestern the most considerate I have ever met. Mr. Omer made our stay in Evanston very enjoyable, and I can assure all that a visiting athlete will be given the best of treatment and every courtesy at his hands. He and Mr. Roe are good friends, and I hope that it will be my privilege to compete at another Northwestern meet.

Upon my return home the people welcomed me as the upholder of the athletic reputation of the school and town, and we were treated in real championship fashion. The meet gave me the first insight into the tricks and diplomacy of the eastern athlete, and I learned more of the tricks of the running game than I ever dreamed of. I continued to train, and the opening of our outdoor track season found me in the best of condition.

In the Seventh District meet, held at Pratt, Kansas, April 26, I ran the 100-yard dash in 9 4/5 seconds. Three of the six watches gave me a 9 3/5. I won the 50 in 5/25 seconds, equaling the world's record; the 220, 220 hurdles, the broad jump, and the shot-put, with a mark of 46 feet 2 inches. Our school won the meet in easy fashion and I won the individual cup, capturing six first places.

When the meet under the auspices of the University of Kansas were held, the following week, at Lawrence, our men were in the best condition for a hard contest. Lawrence high school had taken great pride in her track team and had won this state meet for eleven consecutive years. It was our ambition to break this winning streak, and when the day of the meet came, we felt we had a good chance. The day was cold, and the rain fell in torrents. I knew that the track would be a sea of mud, destroying any hopes I might have of lowering my records of the year before. Our school piled up the points as fast the events were run; Pattinson, Bates, Freese and Booher winning in the face of fast competition. With our five men we were against 22 representing Lawrence, and fast bunches from all parts of the state. I felt cold and stiff from the rain, but the coach and the rest of us were fighting for points, and even a third place could not be overlooked. I won the 50, 100, 220, 220 hurdles, broad jump and shot-put; Pattinson won the pole vault and all of the men seconds and thirds. When the final count was made, just before the relay, it was found that we needed to win at least second place in the relay to take the meet. Pattinson, Booher, Freese and Bates easily accomplished this, and we went home with the trophy cup and individual cup, feeling that all of our hard training and work was well worthwhile. The meet gave us the track championship of the state of Kansas.

One of the fastest meets in which I ever ran was that at Wichita, under the auspices of Fairmount College. We won the meet in easy style in Class A, there being 250 athletes, from 35 schools. All of our men won points and we took at least one place in every event, showing the versatility of our men. Pattinson won the pole vault, Freese was second in javelin, Donnell second in the half. I had little difficulty in getting five firsts and the individual. We were treated royally by Fairmount College and were glad we had voted to go to this meet instead of the one at Manhattan. I might state that it was through the generosity of Coach Roe that we were enabled to enter this meet, and also the one at Lawrence. This concluded our track schedule, we thought of breaking training when Coach Roe told us that he was going to try to take us to Stagg's great meet in Chicago in June. It seemed too good to be true, but we kept at work, feeling that "even that was possible."

In recognition of the work of our team, the Hutchinson businessmen and the Class of 1914 contributed most of the money which enabled us to take the trip to Chicago, where Hutchinson won second place in Stagg's big meet, June 13. A committee composed of Coach Roe, Earnest Freese and Norval Sifers worked hard to make this trip possible. Thanks to the generosity of Lewis Omer, of Evanston, we spent five days in the lake country before the day of the meet and had every chance to be in good form. We trained on Northwestern field and felt that we were acclimated. When the long, anticipated day arrived, it began to rain. A

nd we knew that we would have to fight on another heavy track. We were neither daunted by the weather or the stories of "dark horses." There were 500 athletes, representing 99 schools, at the meet. They came from nearly every state in the union, and, from the talk, "they were all ten second men." I realized that I would have to go up against men who had been in fast competition for several years, but I believed that I would make a good account of myself. The preliminaries were runoff in record time, and many a good man lost out through luck, the inability to pick an opening, or through getting boxed. As the meet progressed the boys of our team ran well, but, like most of the visitors, most of them failed to place. Pattinson tied for sixth place in the pole vault, and Whittaker, the plucky little runner from Nickerson, won a fourth in the quarter.

When the finals in the 100 were finally called I found that I would have to run against Carter, the crack sprinter of Chicago University high school. He had a record of ten flat and was certainly a splendid sprinter. Although there were other good men in the race, everyone was watching us because we had made the best time in the preliminaries. We toed the line in the face of a slight wind and the chilling rain. After several false starts we were off with all the power we had, in really the race of the day. We ran even until about the last 25 yards, when I left him by a final burst of speed and crossed the tape three feet ahead. The time was 10 flat, which, considering the condition of the track, was more than I had hoped for.

In the final of the 220-yard dash Carter evened up with me by beating me by about the same distance, in a hard race. I placed in the 220 hurdles, but when the time came to run the finals I was suffering severely from chills and cramps, caused by the chilling rain and severe exertion. I easily won the broad jump with a leap of 21 feet and 11 ½ inches, taken off in the mud. I was a foot and ten inches ahead of the nearest man in this event. I was very well satisfied with having won four cups, the first in the 100, second in the 220, first in the broad jump, and the magnificent individual cup. The greatest honor was in having Hutchinson in second place out of 99 schools. It seemed that all my years of training were not in vain.

Following the meet all of the visiting athletes were entertained by the students of Chicago University in the common rooms on the campus. In the evening the cups were presented by Coach Stagg and the officials in charge of the meet. I was honored by being called to the platform to say a few words in behalf of our team and our school.

There were cups given for the first five places, all just alike except in size, the first-place trophies being the largest. Being anxious to get in touch with athletes near Chicago, I decided to stay in Evanston for the summer with Coach Roe, who was planning to be with John R. Richards, superintendent of sports and playgrounds in the parks of South Chicago. During the time I spent in Evanston I had a chance to see the crack runners of the country in action, many of them taking part in the meets given by several of the athletic clubs. A good number of my friends wanted to me to run in these meets, and I finally decided to enter the Chicago Athletic club meet at Grant Park in August. It was here that I ran against Joe Loomis, one of the best men in the country and winner of the 100-yard event in the National AAU at Baltimore last year. Loomis and I both won our heats in the preliminaries and when it came to the finals in the 120-yard dash, the interest was great. I had never run this race and wasn't just sure of the pace I had to set; but resolved to do my best. The judges decided finally that Loomis had won first place by a few inches. I hope to meet Loomis again at some future date. On account of the decision being very unsatisfactory to a good many people who claimed that I had won, both on account of the photo taken of the finish and the disagreement of the judges, I challenged Loomis to another race, but up the present time we have had no chance to meet again. Still, I have nothing but praise for "Shorty," for he is fair and square, and a magnificent runner.

When I began to see the exceptional chances for an athlete in Illinois, I decided that I would attend school somewhere in the state the following year. About this time my coach, Mr. H. N. Roe, accepted a position as director of athletics in the schools of Rock Island. I soon afterward asked my coach if he would care if I wrote to the superintendent there to see if there was a good chance for me to help pay my way, and if my brother Ben would have a chance. Both Mr. Roe and Mr. Fisher were agreeable to the plan. I was anxious to continue my work under Coach Roe, as he had developed me and gave me a chance to compete in higher athletics. A good many people wonder why I came to Rock Island to attend school. It was simply a case of deep gratitude and friendship I feel for Mr. Roe and the desire to stay with him, together with my plan for running in the bigger meets in the middle west. I could have gone to many other schools and, perhaps, have gotten along better, but I picked Rock Island for the reasons I have mentioned.

Rock Island is a real live town and supports all kinds of athletics. Still for several years, championship teams had not been developed. At the beginning of the football season Coach Roe started out to produce a winning football team. To say the least, it was a slow and tough proposition. The boys of the high school, up to this year, have not had the advantage of playing grade football, consequently all the knowledge of the game that they get has to begin with their high school course. In Kansas the boys play football in the sixth grade, and when they are candidates for a real team, they know a lot about the game. Inexperience was the great enemy of our work last season and a lot of the men had to be developed. All of the thirty men who stayed out for the greater part of the season were hard workers and everyone did his best. That some were better than others, was due to previous experience rather than to natural superiority. Some of the men just began to train when the season started, when it should be the policy of every athlete who expects to endure a season of football to start in the middle of the summer. Still when we met the Alumni in the first game of the season, we handed them a defeat by one touchdown, in a hard-fought game. The second game was with Aledo, a team which proved easy. We ran up a score of 76-0 in a game that proved to be more of a farce than a real contest.

Our team developed slowly, though Coach Roe and Captain Hinckley worked hard with the men. A number of players who had been out of school for a year came back to help make the season a success. The town became interested in the team and there was said to be more spirit than had been shown in the city for several years. We went along very well until we met Rockford—dear old Rockford—they treated us so nicely and beat us so fairly that I recall the game with a feeling half of fond recollection and sad remembrance. We went to Rockford in the highest of spirits, and, honestly, when the game started, we felt pretty good. We held them for about five minutes, or just so long as we worked as a team. Then something seemed to go wrong and, although the boys fought bravely, we were doomed to defeat. The teamwork that we had been working hard to develop was not there, and from that moment our work spelled defeat for us. A machine cannot go smoothly when the main cog is missing, and we were 'short a cog' at Rockford. Every man on the team played his best; but playing your best does not produce results s well as playing together.

After the game the "I Told You So" bunch got together and held meetings in different pool halls of the city. They blamed our defeat to first one player and then another; but one prophet, more wise than the rest, described it when he said, "the reason Rock Island lost was because Rockford had a red coat band which continued to play 'Nearer My God to Thee,' and this made the home team invincible." I listened to the arguments and, solemn as I am, I was forced to laugh now and then. Another member of the I-T-Y-S said that he used to live in Rockford, and while was talking he became so excited that his emotion became contagious and he finally told this story:
"Every member of the Rockford team attends Sunday school regularly, and some even sing in the choir."

At the conclusion of this statement I realized that like Postum, "There's a Reason." Yes, they played like Christians and their endurance was superb. Perhaps Zeus, the God of strength and valor of a clean heart and person, had become offended at the conduct of some of our players and had taken vengeance upon us in the form of a defeat at the hands of those more in his favor.

In my few years of travel I have learned to weigh the conversation of people on any subject, and if there is in the crowd anyone who seems not to have the proper endowment of grey matter, you can depend upon him to always stumble upon the central thought. This it was my observation in the case of the I-T-Y-S congregation. It is an evident fact that clean living produces strength, valor and manhood, while clean minds and morals of the parents of high ideals, unselfishness, modesty and fair-mindedness. Enough of this for I must go on with the story.

The next football game was in the nature of a track meet with a little more excitement than that of the Aledo game. Ottawa took the goose egg of a 53-0 score. The substitutes all had a good chance to distinguish themselves. In the Monmouth game, which followed, we nearly ran ourselves to death chasing up and down the field. The score was 73 to 0, and the tremendous work of the weeks following the Rockford game was surely evident in the playing of the men. Our loyal crowd of supporters, both in the school and the town, came out to see us practice, and many said that it was more interesting than the game. If all football contests were like the game with Monmouth the Athletic Association would have to give a premium with every ticket to draw a crowd. Too many easy games tend to give a team overconfidence, and I have always thought that it was better lose a close game fairly than to defeat a far weaker team by a very large score. The next game was at Princeton, where we enjoyed the freedom and excitement usually found in a little, strictly temperance, town. The Princeton team was lighter bunch than ourselves; but certainly speedy. They uncorked a little surprise for us during the first five minutes of play. They were ardent exponents of the Minnesota shift, with lots of trick play, and then completely bewildered our boys for a while. They used this shift to perfection and continued to make gains of 10 and 15 yards every down until they had carried the ball over for a touchdown. They kicked goal and the score stood 7 to 0 at the start of the game. On the next kick off I got the ball on our 15 yard line and ran the length of the field for a touchdown and Gleason kicked goal. By this time our boys had solved the secret of the shift, and from that time on Princeton was at our mercy. The final score was 27 to 7. In order that some of the readers will understand the nature of the next game, I will say that Rock Island is located in the northwest portion of Illinois, with Moline adjoining its corporate limits and Davenport, Iowa, directly across the Mississippi River. These cities are known as the Tri-Cities and are friendly rivals in business and athletics. The rivalry among the several schools is intense and all are ever struggling for supremacy.

All season long we had looked forward to the game with Davenport. Although not in the state, we wanted to do our best and win if our light team and limited experience would allow it. Here lies a sad story, and even as I write the date, Nov. 11, it seems that it will always be a rather sad day with me. Davenport is noted for being a German center, while Moline has a large Swedish population, and Rock Island is largely cosmopolitan. When we crossed the Mississippi and invaded the territory of the Germans to do battle on the football field our warriors were valiant and full of confidence, and the non-combatants were many and noisy. Davenport's soldiers were heavy men, outweighing us at least ten pounds to the man. Besides they had plenty of speed in Kelly and Tomson. When it came to weight, "Fat" Thompson at center was a human dreadnaught of two hundred pounds displacement. Shuler was a good combination of weight, strength and aggressiveness. Our team had fighting spirit, was well trained and well coached, but had not enough endurance to stand against the heavier opponents. When the game started the Germans tried to outflank us, but our speed cut short his hope of attack. General Kelly then resorted to his heavy artillery, Tomson and Shuler. By recklessly bombarding our center they drove us straight before them and crossed our goal for a touchdown after several minutes of play. Our fighting blood was up, just like the blood of the European allies at the present time. We fought hard but what could do against the heavy odds. When we again kicked off the Germans made another "march of triumph." We contested every inch of ground, but to no avail. Finally, when within our closer defenses, one of the enemy's shot failed to explode and the ball was fumbled. One of our men fell on the ball and we were safe for the time. I was playing quarterback and I did some hard thinking to decide where to make the advance. When the center covered the ball, we were so close to the goal that our back field was across the goal line. I called for a punt formation, but I saw my wall of defense ready to crumble and perhaps allow the enemy to down me before I could punt. I decided to take my chance on a long end run. I knew that if I could get across the line of scrimmage, I could hold my own with the speed of the Davenporters. The ball was quickly passed into my hands and I started around left end. As I crossed the line, dodging this way and that, I resolved never to stop until I had made a touchdown, if it was in me to do it. I saw Kelly coming toward me running low, and I knew he was a sure tackler. I increased my speed to the utmost, and just as he dove for my legs, I swerved a little and he missed me by a few inches. On my left I saw Tomson heading for me, but I thought that I could outrun him, which I succeeded in doing. I crossed the goal line and Gleason kicked goal. The Rock Island grandstand went wild, and I have never heard such enthusiasm at a high school game.

There are times when a certain mental strain seems to affect a team, keeping the men from doing the right thing at the right time. When we received the ball on the kick-off, we were not the same team that had fought so hard a short time before. Nevertheless, we put up a stiff fight and the boys deserve a whole lot of credit for the way they worked. Cliff Whisler, Joel Nichols, Ray Crisswell and Bob Ackley played wonderfully well that game. Some of the I-T-Y-S crowd said we might have won the game, but I know that every man fought hard for the honor of the school and the town. When a team can 'come back' and win after a disheartening defeat, it is the test of the men and of the coach. It can be truthfully said that there was not a mistake made in the Davenport game that we did not profit by when we met Moline in the fastest game of the season the following Saturday. Before a great crowd of 4000 people we played wonderful football. Certain shifts in our lineup had greatly strengthened the team, and we easily won the most coveted game of the football year. Coach Roe put me at end, with Nichols beside me. Together we kept the Swedes guessing as to whether it was going to be a forward pass or a line buck. Bob Ackley, Whisler and Gaetjer in turn took the ball across tackle for good gains and our line held like a wall. Little "Toughy" Johnson, at quarter, ran the team like a veteran, and finally, when "Fighting Bill" Gleason took Bob's place, we ripped Moline's forwards to pieces and crossed our opponent's goal line for the first time in three years. The crowd was in ecstasy, and Gleason, who carried the ball across and also kicked goal, was the happiest man in the country. Every man worked hard. Looby at end, Culley at center, and in fact every man on the team. Morris, one of the hardest working players I ever knew, was put in the game and quickly made another touchdown, which failed to count. I dived over the line for a second touchdown near the close of the second half. As I walked off the field, I realized how happy I was, and felt with the poet:

> "Whichever way the wind doth blow,
>
> Some heart is glad to have it so.
>
> Then blow it east or blow it west,
>
> The wind that blows—that wind is best!"

At the present time I am playing basketball with the school team. I greatly enjoy the sport; and had the satisfaction of playing in the game where we won from Moline in this indoor sport. Captains Reeves, Morris, Gleason, Rinck, Culley, Hinkley and Whisler are all fine players, and we hope to win the Galesburg tournament. Mr. Cook, Mr. Robb, and Coach Roe have all helped in training the team, and it is safe to say that we will stand high in this branch of sport.

I am looking forward to a good track season and will work hard to be in better form that I ever was before. I will always do my very best for Rock Island.

There will be a revised edition of this work at the conclusion of the period dating from the opening of the basketball season up to the ending of the term in May.

In closing this book, I would like to make you acquainted with Mr. A.J. Burton, the principal of the high school. Mr. Burton is a man whom I admire for his integrity, his high ideals and fair-mindedness. It is interesting and valuable to know the people with whom you come in contact; therefore, I have made a study of Mr. Burton's character, and I am sure the he has the interests of the school at heart. He means well by every student in the school, and those who think that he does not have only to know him to think differently. The principal of any high school ha a great deal to endure, and there are always persons who think that it is their duty to run the school instead of performing the duties that fall upon them. I have every reason to like Mr. Burton, and I greatly appreciate the many courtesies that he has shown both my brother and myself. Rock Island should be glad to have him as one of its foremost educators.

As I introduce Mr. E. C. Fisher, the superintendent, I think of the number of social gatherings we have had in the high school and the clever stories that he has told. I think he is one of the best speakers I have ever listened to. His talks give you ideas that can help you in future life if you will put them into practice. He is a man who realizes that you can't make old people out of young ones; that boys will be boys, and that there is a good side to every one's life. Mr. Fisher is a general favorite with the students and a very popular man among the people of the Tri-Cities.

I hardly need to make you acquainted with Mr. Herbert N. Roe, the man who has done most in my development. He is a wonderful coach and has a most inspiring personality. You have met him on the field, track and gym, and also in the intellectual affairs of the school. Mr. Roe is the man who enabled me to reach my place in athletics and to compete with the foremost athletes in the United States. I have proven, and I hope to continue to do so, that the Roe system of coaching and training is always good. He studies each man and always get the very best out of his material. As he has an athletic record himself, he knows how to treat his men and how much to demand of them. A number of athletes go on the field to win fame when they haven't done the right thing up to the time they compete. Then when they find that they cannot produce the goods they lay the blame on the coach. A coach is the same as a teacher, he can instruct you, but you must learn for yourself. Besides, if you are not interested in your work you are a failure. Mr. Roe and I have worked together for more than two years, and I more than appreciate what he has done for me in my struggle for recognition and success. I hope to be able to prove to the world in the Pan-American meet the Coach H.N. Roe is in every sense 'a real coach." He has given me for a motto, "Always finish the race a yard beyond the tape," also "It is not wealth, or rank, or state, But 'Get up and get' that makes men great."

How I run the dashes

In running the short dashes, the main object is to get off ahead of the other fellow without jumping the gun and getting set back. To accomplish this, you must be cool headed and quick. I try to make my starts a matter of reflex action and depend upon the gun for the impetus. During my entire career I have never jumped the gun. When I am training for a race, I have brother or coach to start me in every way imaginable. I do this, for every starter has his own idea of the way athletes should get off, and some hold you longer than others. The best starters I have ever run under are, in my mind, Hamilton of Kansas University, and Cayuse, at Northwestern.

50-yard dash

In the fifty, it is necessary to give every ounce of strength from the very start, hurling yourself at the tape when nearing the finish.

100-yard dash

The century is the greatest race known to the track, and supremacy in this is coveted by a great many sprinters. The start should be as quick as possible, every muscle in the lower part of the body in action on the instant. The chest muscles should be relaxed until within fifteen yards from the finish. At this point you must have something in reserve, gauging your strength so that you can increase your stride near the tape. The last fifteen yards determines the winner in a close race, your power of concentration and determination counting for a great deal. The length of your stride depends on yourself and the manner in which you run. Some fast men use short strides while other use very long ones.

220-yard dash

This race is run a little differently from the 100, but you must keep in mind the two essentials of the first race. You should run the 220 with the real finish starting about fifty yards from the finish. To do this you will have to gauge your strength accordingly. The first fifty yards should be run at high speed to rid yourself of the fastest opponents and enable you to cut in if you are running on a curve. After you have done this, settle down to an even gai, always keeping your competitors within three yards of you. Some of them will misjudge their strength before they have gone

120 yards. During this time, you be left for three yards, but never let any man get more than that distance ahead of you. When you reach the fifty-yard mark give the very best you have in you to the final leap for the tape. To do this you must have confidence in yourself, absolutely no fear, and be willing to lose if there is a better man in the race. If you have confidence, the time that you might spend shivering with fear or nervousness you can spend in studying the men who are to be your opponents.

220 hurdles

Of all the races that I run I like the hurdles the best. There is lots of real enjoyment in leaping these barriers. It is sport from the crack of the gun to the finish. It requires a lot of hard practice to be able to get over the hurdles properly and to keep an even stride between them, also never to 'float' them. The nearer you come to clearing the bars without knocking them over, the better. This is what every coach and athlete calls 'form.' To develop this form, you must have a weak mind and strong shins. I think I have neither, so I have never mastered this form. I just get over them and trust to my speed to get me to the tape first. I have never been beaten in a hurdle race.

The other races, from the 440 up to the marathons, are tests of endurance rather than skill or form. I have often run the 440, and it is the hardest of all races. It demands great endurance and moderate speed.

Method of training

A painter once asked his teacher how to mix his paints. "With brains, sir," was the reply. This answer can be substituted in the process of training.

There are no two athletes in the world alike, and every man has to study himself, and devise his own system of training. His muscular development should be studied, and natural ability developed along the line that his is best fitted for. There are some set rules that we have to follow if we desire to make good, namely: right living, a proper mental attitude, proper food and sufficient rest, all combined with hard work. As for the food question, I eat reasonable amounts of wholesome food with very little fatty or sweet stuff. I always have regular meal hours and never eat a thing between meals. If possible, before every strenuous contest I drink a glass of milk and a raw egg in it. This is easily digested, and I think helps my wind. Another thing is very refreshing to me is ice cream, and I hardly get enough of it. On the day of a meet I take a hearty breakfast of some kind of meat, toast, eggs, and milk and at noon two eggs, some toast and one glass of milk. Dieting is worth something, but proper rest is much more so. I usually go to bed around 10 o'clock and never later than 10:30 and always get up at seven. Too much sleep is as bad as not enough. On the night before a meet or hard game I always retire at 10 o'clock and I always adhere to this set rule. When my friends say to me, "Come on with us, you will get in in plenty of time," I tell them that to make good, an athlete must sacrifice pleasure and attend strictly to business. If I fooled around till midnight before a contest my friends would be the first to say, "I knew Sol couldn't stay up all night and win." On the other hand, if I am beaten, all they can say is that I trained hard but was beaten by a better man. When I go to a meet, I always take my brother Ben with me, because he is proof against all doubts and fears and has unlimited confidence in my ability. When we start for a meet Ben takes a program and decides on the events that I am expected to win.

"Look, Sol! We will win this." He always says "we," on account of his past achievements, when he used to outrun me any day in the week. Sometimes I think my brother believes I could make a watch with a sledgehammer. His good humor and laughter are so contagious that soon I find myself running imaginary races and coming out as Ben predicts.

The only time that Ben's judgment was poor was at the indoor meet at Northwestern last March. I had placed in six events the first night, which was no small task, on account of my not being acclimated nor accustomed to working indoors. After winning the broad jump and the sixty yard dash, Mr. Omer advised me to pass up the 440 in order to be in good shape for the sixty yard hurdles, but Ben insisted that I run in order that the people wouldn't think me a quitter. When he hinted that, it was more than I could stand, and I lined up with the rest of the quarter milers. Before that race was over I had accumulated a thousand dollars-worth of experience. I did not even place in it and at every stride I learned something new about using my arms, about getting pocketed and the finer points of this kind of a race. After the race I had about ten minutes to get ready for the hurdles and was very tired. Ben said, "don't mind, Sol, they know you are not a quitter, besides every athlete has to be beaten once in a while." He continued to console me until by the time he had finished the rub down I was proud to hear him say, "Sol, I have added five points more for Hutchinson, go out and claim them for me."

After the meet Ben decided that if I had kept out of the quarter, I could have raised my feet a little higher and avoided knocking over the hurdle which disqualified me and knocked me out of a world's record. Nevertheless, I hope to have Ben's prediction come true, that I will do these things when I compete again at Northwestern. Not every athlete is so fortunate as to have an enthusiastic brother as a constant companion.

Sol had hoped that the sales of this book would be enough to support his goal of attending Harvard. Sadly, sales did not live up to his expectations. The addendum to this book about his senior year track season never materialized.

About the author

I was born in Centerville, Iowa but was raised in Rock Island, Illinois and attended public schools there, graduating from Rock Island Senior High School in 1979. I was co-editor of *The Crimson Crier*, the school newspaper and was on the staff of the school's yearbook, <u>WatchTower</u>. I attended Black Hawk College in Moline, Illinois and graduated with an Associate Degree in Journalism, and was also the editor of *The Chieftain*, the weekly college paper. I worked at Iowa-Illinois Gas and Electric Company, and later Mid-American Energy Company for 38 years before retiring. Another local history project very dear to me was when I was asked to collaborate with Doug Frazer and Rick Miers, both RIHS alums, on a book on the history of Rock Island High School. The book, <u>Rock Solid-Our History</u>, is an exclusive book on its history, dating from 1857 to present. It featured interesting stories related to the school, plus was jam-packed with many photos. Because of that book, I realized that the Solomon Butler story needed to be told. While working on the Butler book, I began doing research related to the history of Rock Island High School's football and basketball teams. Finally realizing it was a daunting task, I asked fellow classmate Jeff Wendland to do the writing for both books. I have enjoyed collecting hundreds of photographs for both books to help document the history of these two sports. I also enjoy photography, mainly taking images of old barns, old cars, and bald eagles, and in 2022, had a photo of mine selected to become a US postage stamp in a series called the Mighty Mississippi River, and in 2023, a photo was a finalist of the Iowa PBS contest, Iconic Iowa.

Made in the USA
Columbia, SC
10 July 2024

38436676R00130